I0115811

COMMENTS ABOUT THE 2nd EDITION OF THE BOOK

Wayne Frye has written another blistering exposé on American hypocrisy. In this 2nd edition of the book, he parades out a group of individuals who have suffered mightily at the hands of American leaders who want to stifle all dissent in their obsession to program the compliant American populace to do the bidding of those who would enslave all of humanity to corporate dominated capitalism, patriotic servitude and religious bigotry........*Cue Blog*

Wayne Frye is an American expatriate who looks with cold, calculating clarity at what is today the single greatest threat to true democratic values and social justice for the teaming masses of the world. This behemoth of corporate, military and moral hypocrisy is the United States of America......................*W.W. Bachman*

Wayne Frye's father and uncles served in World War II and as a freedom loving patriot, he volunteered to serve during the Vietnam War. However, it was not combat duty that would profoundly change his political views. Eventually assigned to the Pentagon, where he became privy to top-secret information, he began to discern the real America that is hidden from the populace. Seeing the subterfuge, the conniving, the suppression of groups and countries that were trying to bring social justice to citizens made him realize that he had been fed a steady diet of lies by the government and corporate media. Within a short time, he came to the realization that it was not the Viet Cong or the communists who were the American people's enemies, but rather, it was their own government. These same deceptive practices continue today, and in this book, Dr. Frye lays bare the cold, hard facts of America's suppression of dissent........... *Library Review*

This is a gripping tale of woe that reads like a novel and will keep you on the edge of your seat. How America strives to suppress dissent and control people makes you realize that we must all be eternally vigilant to make sure the social democracies of the world do not slip into the same American pattern of oppression and manipulation that puts, not only freedom of speech at peril, but will make all of us slaves to the corporate bottom line that is the real power in America, which fuels its war machine and poverty gulag..*International Herald*

ABOUT THE AUTHOR

Wayne Frye is from the small town of Asheboro, North Carolina, where he grew up in the 1950's and 60's. Although a product of a society that was insular and resisted social change, through the influence of his liberal minded grandmother, he developed a social consciousness that made him acutely aware of the oppressive nature of a segregated society. Leaving that society to serve in the military during the Vietnam War, and to attend several universities, he received his Bachelor's, Master's and Doctoral degrees from institutions that were at the vanguard of the 1960's and 1970's movement toward social justice.

His first book in 1971, *The Loss of the American Dream*, was written while he was the youngest professor at Hunter College (City University of New York). It was particularly popular among activist students in New York and New Jersey. While a professor at Rowan State University, in 1976, he wrote the screenplay and directed *Simba*, an experimental film that became a popular cult classic on college campuses and cable access channels. He spent many years as a college professor and administrator, concentrating on writing textbooks. He was president of universities in Louisiana and Utah. He has been a television producer and director, specializing in educational and distance learning programming. He has also been a restaurateur, a marketing consultant and university hockey coach. In 2003, after spending many years directing an intensive academic support program for ghetto children in South-central Los Angeles, he immigrated to an idyllic Canadian island (Vancouver Island) in search of what he calls a more equalitarian, just and compassionate society. Since 2005, his Aaron Adams novels have been a favourite of Canadian mystery readers. He and his wife, Jasmine, who also, on occasion, writes with him, live in the small seaside community of Ladysmith, British Columbia.

FIGHTING FOR JUSTICE

OTHER BOOKS BY J. WAYNE FRYE

TEXTBOOKS

Introduction to Advertising
. Promotions Workbook
. Mastering Marketing Research
Advertising Design
Guide to Local Radio-Television Copywriting
Marketing Plan Workbook
Public Relations Workbook

NON-FICTION

The Loss of the American Dream
Cataclysmic Dreams in Black and White
The Catastrophic Calamities of a Village Idiot
Guide to Alternative Education (13 Editions)
Fighting for Justice in the Land of Hypocrisy
How Hockey Saved a Jew From The Holocaust

NON-FICTION BOOKS WITH JASMINE FRYE

Canadian Angels of Mercy: Nurses in Times of Peril
Points of Rebellion: North American Aboriginals Who Fought for Justice

NOVELS

The Fall From Apocalypse
Armageddon Now
Something Evil in the Darkness at Hopkins House
When Jesus Came to Jersey as the Son of Thunder
Hockey Mania and the Mystery of Nancy Running Elk
The Girl Who Stirred Up the Whirlwind (Coming Soon)

**The non-textbooks listed above are available
at your local bookstore or from Amazon.com**

FIGHTING FOR JUSTICE

10987654321

First Edition Copyright 2007
by
J. Wayne Frye
2nd Edition Copyright 2012
by
J. Wayne Frye

All rights reserved. No part of this book may be
reproduced or transmitted in any form or by any other
means, electronic or mechanical, including
photocopying, recording, or by any information
storage and retrieval system, without permission from
the author.

Catalogue Number: 20075186209

ISBN: 978-0-9735973-5-6

Manufactured in Canada

Peninsula Publishing / Colony Publishing
Distributes Books Under the Following Labels:
Adams Books   Incredible Stories
Australian Literary Classics Canadian Literary Classics
Fireside Books   Olympia Books

Fireside Books
Distribution Centre NA
#1 Adams Place, Suite M-16
Victoria, BC V9B 6P6

FIGHTING FOR JUSTICE IN THE LAND OF HYPOCRISY

by
J. Wayne Frye

PROFILES IN COURAGE ABOUT THOSE
WHO HAVE FOUGHT AND THOSE WHO
ARE STILL FIGHTING
THE FORCES OF OPPRESSION IN THE
FALSE AMERICAN DEMOCRACY THAT
ATTEMPTS TO PROMULGATE
UNIFORMITY ON ITS POPULACE

NOTE: This book is written in Canadian
English, so teachers using the publisher's
vocabulary list should alert students to the
differences in spellings.

FIGHTING FOR JUSTICE

"Those unwilling to demand their rights,
don't deserve any." – Wayne Frye (1970)
(Photo from Civil Rights Archives – In Public Domain)

"The authorities will always defend the status-quo,
because it is the status-quo that gives them
their pay check and their power." – Wayne Frye (1992)
(Photo in public domain, taken from:
http://learning.blogs.nytimes.com/2012/03/07/march-7-1965-
civil-rights-marchers-attacked-in-selma/)

FIGHTING FOR JUSTICE

TABLE OF CONTENTS

FIGHTING FOR JUSTICE

TO: Ann Powell, my 12th grade English teacher who showed me the power of words, and taught me to question authority in a society that tried to make all its citizens conform. She was truly a teacher who made a difference in my life and the lives of all her students.

JWF

IN MEMEMORIUM

While writing this book, one of my biggest fans (it is easy to define a big fan when you have as few readers as I do) passed away at the age of 83. My beloved Aunt Willa Mae Cagle was a defining force for good in my life, and it is with deep sadness that I realize she will not be around to read this book, and discuss it with me in our bi-weekly phone conversations that had become such an important part of my life after I left America. Knowing she will not be reading my books, certainly makes writing them much less enjoyable. JWF – (From 2007 Edition)

FIGHTING FOR JUSTICE

PROLOGUE
LOCK 'UM UP AND HOUND THEM
INTO OBSCURITY

When I wrote the first edition of this book in 2007, I had freed myself through immigration from the Bush corporate-military fascism that had gripped the USA since his appointment to the presidency by the Supreme Court in 2000. I always find it ironic that a nation can call itself a democracy, but still allow no less than four men to be elected president in its history who actually lost the popular vote (Adams, Hayes, Harrison and Bush). Is not a democracy ruled by the majority?

Watching Bush and his henchmen use fear-mongering to get re-elected in 2004 (maybe with some additional nefarious manipulation of the vote in Ohio, as they had done in Florida in 2000) made me realize that I had made the right decision in voting with my feet in 2003 and becoming a Canadian citizen.

Yet, as an American expatriate, I still have attachments to my native land, but each day those attachments continue to subside, as I grow accustomed to the real freedom offered by a socialistic democracy like Canada. Unfortunately, I often see Canada slipping into the privatization mania and corporate coddling that has made America a land of class distinction, where the haves exercise absolute power over the have-nots.

Most Americans live in denial. They are too wrapped up in patriotic babble, religious subterfuge and capitalistic dogma to see that their country has the least freedom of any democracy on the planet.

How much freedom do you have when an employer can arbitrarily fire you for no reason? How much freedom do you have when you can lose your life-savings and your home, because you or someone in your family has the misfortune to become seriously ill? How much freedom do you have when you have to choose between eating or buying the prescription medicine you need to survive? How much freedom do you have when the FBI can monitor your reading habits at the local library or listen in on your telephone conversations? How much freedom do you have when your elected representatives are in the pockets of the corporate barons of greed who represent the real government? How much freedom do you have when you can be arrested for voicing sympathy with an organization deemed a threat to the state? How much freedom do you have when religion is afforded special dispensation in public forums? How much freedom do you have when the rich and powerful are taxed at a preferential rate, while the middle class bears the burdens of supplying minimal welfare for the poor and lavish welfare for the rich? How much freedom do you have when corporations make billions, but expect their workers to take pay cuts to keep them competitive in an economy dominated by the giant capitalistic monoliths of exploitation? How much freedom do you have when lavish salaries and benefits are afforded government officials while the common person is told to sacrifice for the good of the country? How much freedom do you have when the government that supposedly represents you allows its agents to engage in the torture of those who would stand against it? How much freedom do you have when a few religious demagogues are given access to the halls of power in a government that is supposed to be non-sectarian? How much freedom do you have when corporations that are more interested in the bottom line than the public welfare run the television networks? How much freedom do you have when vast sums of money are spent to maintain a war machine while domestic needs are neglected? How much freedom do you have when??????????????????????????????????????

America is a land of broken promises and dreams, as years of hope have been allowed to flow into a river of mediocrity. There have been times when America almost changed, when some social justice crept into a system based on greed, but always, in the end, the rich and powerful somehow managed to wrest control from those who wanted to alter the system of capalistic servitude that has now spread around the world in the form of globalization to snare billions in the evil web of corporate slavery.

The Great Depression showed the folly of the capitalistic system of greed, and, had it not been for Franklin Roosevelt, probably America's greatest President, capitalism would have perished as people would have risen up against a system of servitude that is just as insidious as the serfdom practiced in the Middle Ages. So, ironically, the corporations should be thankful to a Democrat, who instituted social programs in order to save the country from the anarchy that the Republicans were willing to let occur, rather than reach out with a helping hand to the millions put in dire circumstances by the system of capitalistic greed to which they gave free reign, which eventually led to the tumultuous stock market crash that brought on the Great Depression and finally the great economic meltdown of 2008.

President Herbert Hoover represents the heartless attitude that is at the very core of Republican Party principles. During the height of the Depression, 40,000 starving World War I veterans descended on Washington, DC in mass to demand the war bonuses they were promised, so they could put bacon and beans on the table for their families, while the President dined on caviar at the White House. The men who had served their country were just malcontents according to Hoover, so he ordered troops in to disperse them. Lead by another great Republican, Douglas MacArthur, who made himself a war hero while skipping out on his men in the Philippines; the protestors were heartlessly attacked by sabre wielding brutes on horseback.

Ironically, this party of cold, heartless, corporate loving hypocrites is, today, considered the moral party, and receives nearly unanimous support from Fundamentalist Christians. These Christians seem to think the key to solving all the world's problems is Jesus Christ. They are the same people who unabashedly support Israel in its conflict with the Palestinians, because they are God's chosen people. Paradoxically, they also preach that Jews will not be in heaven unless they accept Jesus Christ. They are the same pack of hypocrites who wanted to impeach Bill Clinton for lying about trysts with Monica Lewinsky,

12   IN THE LAND OF HYPOCRISY

but were content to let George "Bring Um On" Bush escape impeachment for lying about weapons of mass destruction in Iraq. This hypocrisy is at the very core of what the Republican Party and its right wing Christian supporters are all about.

Since the founding of America by a group businessmen and gentleman farmers who wanted to avoid paying taxes to England, the USA has been a nation of hypocrisy. How else can you account for the framers of the Constitution declaring, "all men are created equal" while the majority of the individuals writing that phrase were slaveholders. Likewise, it is interesting that they used the word men, as there were no women signers of the Constitution. Women were denied the right to vote until 1920.

I was reared on a steady diet of American patriotism. As a child, most of the adult men I knew were veterans of World War II. I can remember men who were legless, armless, blind or walking around with plates in their heads. Many of them lived on the margins of the capitalistic society they defended. One legless man, in particular, I remember as the individual who sat on the street selling pencils. I always felt compelled to buy my school pencils for five cents from him rather than the store, because my Dad told me it was the right thing to do. I hardly knew the man, other than a casual hello, but one day when I wanted pencils and he was not there on his usual corner, I actually cried when I heard that he had died. He also had a plate in his head, and apparently, the wartime injury to his brain caused his death many years afterward. It took weeks for me to get over his death as, even at the tender age of 6 or

7, I thought how cruel that someone who gave his all for his country had to resort to selling pencils on a street corner to make a living. I could not put my finger on the problem, but even then, I think, subconsciously, I knew that there was something wrong in a system that reduced a patriot to that kind of existence. Where was the fairness? Here was a man who was one of the millions who actually saved American society, and he was just another forgotten patriot who had been used up and discarded. While the barons of greed were making obscene wartime profits, this man had defended their way of life, only to be abused by the system he had saved. Today, there is no draft, so only the marginalized of society are expected to serve. They do the dying to defend democracy, while the offspring of the rich are busy going to college, as they turn their noses up at those of us who actually have to work for a living. Can you actually imagine a George Bush or Mitt Romney on a factory floor actually putting in a real day's work?

My father and most of my uncles served in World War II, and they all had a strong steak of patriotic fervour, but as things changed in America, I saw them start to question what was happening? My own father, many times called me a communist, because I believed that socialism was the only way to create a truly just society, and he was an American success story, so he did not want to countenance any divergence from the free enterprise system. He had difficulty understanding that what America had evolved into was not free enterprise. Free enterprise existed for only a short time in America until all the robber barons got together and froze out the little guy. What America has is corporate enterprise, where 2 or 3 companies control 90% of every market and make it impossible for the small guy to effectively compete. Does anyone really think an individual could open a small town discount store and compete with Wal Mart?

Toward the end of his life, dedicated capitalist that he was, I think my own father began to see the cruelty of a system that had no heart or conscience. He spent one million two hundred thousand dollars on my mother's illnesses after his health insurance ran out. Corporate hospitals often demanded he pay in advance before they would perform the operations necessary to keep her alive. That is the profit motive, which has no place in health care – which should be a human right. I once watched him defiantly count out $80,000 in cash to pay for one operation, and then the hospital administrator told him that they could not accept cash.

My Dad was not one who took kindly to arrogance. After a bombastic outburst and the arrival of security personnel who saw that he was not a man to be travailed with, the administrator thought it might be prudent to accept his offer of a cash payment. In his typical "good old boy" style, my Dad turned to the administrator and said, "you mess with me you arrogant asshole, and I will buy this goddamn place, fire you and tear it down brick by brick." Unfortunately, it was an idle boast, as he did not have the financial means to buy the hospital, even if were for sale, but he made me realize that standing up to authority is often a necessity in a country where people in authority show no compassion for those they are supposed to serve.

FIGHTING FOR JUSTICE

I recall one visit to a hospital where I watched a man sign over a farm that had been in his family for over one hundred years to pay his wife's hospital bill. Meanwhile, the arrogant, flag waving hypocrites of America proclaim it is the greatest country in the world. How can any country as callous and uncaring as America hold itself up as a model to the rest of the world?

Greed is at the very core of human nature, and we are all susceptible to the disease. I abhor Wal Mart and all its stands for as it tries to stifle competition and exploit its workers. Yet, in spite of that disdain, I shop there because of self-interest in getting the lowest price possible. Self- interest is what has put these monoliths of evil in control of the world today. Why don't more workers unionize? The simple answer is that they have been cowered into accepting corporate exploitation, because they are fearful that the corporation will pack up and move elsewhere. For the same reason, we are all caught up in the consumer society that tells us happiness can only be attained by possessing things. Therefore, most individuals live from pay check to pay check, which is exactly what the corporations want, as it keeps their workers fearful of losing their jobs and all the material possessions they make payments on each month.

This devotion to a system of institutionalized greed assures that America will never control immigration on its southern border, as immigration is the life-blood of corporations that depend on immigrant labour to keep wages down. Without the millions of illegal immigrants that pour across the border every year,

FIGHTING FOR JUSTICE

American workers would see the power shift from management to labour. The result would be a working class with power, something that the American government and its corporate controllers will never allow. When Ronald Reagan drove the final nail in organized labour's coffin with the firing of the air traffic controllers, he gave the corporations the green light to exploit workers at will.

I find it particularly ironic that America is so obsessed with terrorists coming in from Canada. They look at Canada as a haven for terrorists, which is understandable. After all, Canada is a truly free country, without the constraints of the fascist-like, draconian Patriot Act that allows the U.S. government to spy on law-abiding citizens. The truth is that Americans are fearful of freedom. They do not realize how repressed their society is. America is at the mercy of a pack of vile, hypocritical, religious, right wing, corporate manipulators who have the people mesmerized with patriotic babble and religious dogma that is spewed out of the mouths of manipulative politicians, CEO's and ministers like water over Niagara Falls.

Meantime, as the American government concentrates on stopping terrorists entering their country from Canada, it does absolutely nothing to stop the flow of people across its southern border; because that would be detrimental to the corporations it serves. Most Arabs are dark skinned and would blend in much easier with the Hispanics coming from Mexico and other countries south of the border than with predominantly white Canadians.

FIGHTING FOR JUSTICE

How many Canadians would stream across the border for a job in crime-ridden, gun-toting, repressive America, where the people work longer hours without the job protections that are a part of Canadian social democracy? The lunacy of this approach to combating terrorism is just another example of an America that is run by a pack of sanctimonious hypocrites who have no concept of what freedom is, and are always looking for another enemy to define. Constantly finding new enemies is the way the American people are controlled.

Recently, a few states have instituted laws targeting illegal aliens, because they are in right-to-work states that have effectively destroyed unions, so that corporations no longer have to depend on illegal immigrants to keep wages low. The governors of these states are using crime as an excuse to racially target immigrants. To them, all the crime is perpetrated by those in the country illegally. Meanwhile, the crimes of the bankers and stock manipulators are of no concern. A man robbing a 7-11 to feed his family is a menace, but a banker or stock broker who steals millions is just an example of good old free enterprise.

The politicians say that other countries are envious of America, which leads to the hatred. The hatred has nothing to do with envy. Talk to the people in Europe, Australia and Canada; they will state categorically that America is not envied, but despised for trying to promulgate its bankrupt ideas of corporate-dominated, capitalistic democracy on the entire world.

One of the best examples of American arrogance is the statement once made by George Bush that terrorists envy America's freedom. What is there to envy? America is a society where there is not even freedom of religion, because freedom of religion also means freedom from religion. Religion is woven into the very fabric of American politics. Why the push to ban gay marriage? Why the preoccupation with abortion? Why did Bush ban stem cell research that could cure millions of debilitating diseases? Why the push to put prayer back in schools? Why the inclusion of prayer at public events? Why the tax exemptions for religious organizations? Why is God's name even in the Pledge of Allegiance? Why is everyone expected to toe the religious line? Why does a lack of religion preclude someone from being elected to public office? In the Unites States of America, religion is indeed the opiate of the masses.

If a place is to be truly democratic like the countries of Europe, Australia and Canada, then no religion can be allowed as part of the fabric of government. Tracing the history of the world, religion has played a part in almost all wars, and every country fighting a war thinks that God is on its side. Even Hitler believed that God had ordained that he and Germany rule the world. Americans sincerely believe that their country is ordained by God to be the beacon of light for the entire planet.

The martyr Dematte said, "religion is the despot's excuse for violence." This is illustrated, not just by the Muslim extremists, but also, by the warmongering Americans, with their weapons of mass destruction, who think that by destroying country after country they are doing God's work. Despots like George Bush and

Dick Cheney have traditionally hidden behind religion while committing crimes against humanity.

America's fundamentalist religious leaders actually have the gall to equate Christianity with capitalism. Nothing could be further from the truth. Does any genuinely caring person think that if there was a Jesus that he would approve of a system that allows the wealthy to pile up riches, while the poor are ignored by a callous, uncaring government that continues to sanction the widening gap between the haves and have-nots?

I am appalled by the religious paragons of virtue who tell me I am doomed to hell, because I do not believe that some 800 year old man got two of every animal in the world on an ark, or that a man actually lived in the belly of a whale. These same virtuous hypocrites laugh at religions that believe in flying elephants or reincarnation. Fairy tales are fairy tales, whether they come from the Bible, the Koran or Mother Goose.

I strongly defend anyone's right to believe whatever she or he wants, but when you start weaving religious beliefs into government, or use them to condemn other's beliefs, then you are guilty of self-righteous arrogance that diminishes everyone's freedom.

The most rewarding job I ever had was with the Los Angeles School District, where I was director of an intensive academic support program for inner city children. However, during the eleven years I was there, I never ceased to be amazed by the intense indoctrination aimed at these children. First, the main goal of the system was not to educate them, but to control them. Discipline was the primary subject that took precedence over all other subjects. The principle goal was to squelch these future anarchists who might bring down the system of institutionalized greed that used them to fuel the machinery of capitalistic exploitation.

The so-called educational leaders emphasized that only by instilling discipline could these miscreants actually begin to learn, and become productive members of society. I just love that phrase, "productive." It goes to the very heart of what education is about in America. Everyone must be taught to work for a corporation, to earn money and to consume. Education is not for esoteric learning; it is all about preparing for a job, a job for the master corporation. Only by serving a corporate master can anyone be truly happy and have access to money, which is at the very root of what makes each one of us worthwhile, according to the American thought process. Happiness is a nice, shiny, new car; or a house in a gated community; or an expensive pair of shoes; or a good meal in an upscale restaurant. Each individual's worth is judged by material possessions. This explains why, when the government settled with the World Trade Centre claimants, the stockbrokers' families received more compensation than the janitors' families. After all, each person had to be judged by his or her earning power. How callous to tell the families of janitors that their husbands, mothers and fathers were not worth as much as the managers, accountants or lawyers. This goes to the core of a capitalistic society, and the way each person's worth is evaluated.

FIGHTING FOR JUSTICE

I tried very hard to make the children I worked with see through this veil of hypocrisy promulgated by a society based on greed. It was a difficult task, as I had to overcome years of capitalistic propaganda that had brainwashed these innocents into believing the only way to judge success was in dollars and cents.

The biggest obstacle in overcoming this brainwashing is presented by corporate controlled television that constantly bombards viewers with the corporate definition of the good life. Most people think that television's purpose is to provide entertainment. Nothing could be further from the truth. Television is nothing but a method of selling goods and services that people do not need to an unsuspecting populace. Entertainment, if today's junk television can be called that, is simply a by-product of advertising. Watching the typical show makes me think that the program is not interrupted by commercials, it is the program that interrupts the commercials. When I was a child, the typical thirty-minute program had three one-minute commercials. I recently counted 27 twenty-second commercials in a thirty minute program. I now tape any program with commercials and watch it later, so that I can zip through the advertisements. Of course, I rarely watch any network comedy program, because the laugh tracks are so pervasive that they interfere with following the storyline, if there is a storyline. I suppose the programmers think they have to brainwash people with a laugh track in order to convince them that their banal attempts at comedy are actually funny. People like Sid Caesar, Jackie Gleason and Milton Berle were talented enough that they did not need laugh tracks. Today's entertainers and writers rely on brainwashing the audience into thinking a program is funny.

Commercials are so pervasive that you even have to sit through several before the film begins at the local theatre today, not to mention, that each film has numerous product placements that often have nothing to do with the plot. I wonder how much the Tobacco Institute pays movie corporations to make sure that most characters smoke in films. A recent survey indicated that around 22% of Americans smoke. However, the same survey found that almost 50% of characters in movies smoke. Canadian figures are slightly less by 4% or 5% in each category.

Capitalism makes every individual nothing more than a consumer. I found it particularly appalling when George Bush and Rudolph Giuliani, after the 9/11 disaster, said the way to show the terrorists they had failed was for people to come to New York City and shop. Along with attacking a country (Iraq) that had nothing to do with 9/11, America's solution to the disaster was to spend money on material things. How crass and barbaric that in the midst of all this agony, pain and anguish; these two representatives of corporate greed waved the flag of capitalism before the dust had cleared from the fallen towers.

Unfortunately, America has exported its particular brand of corporate capitalism to the entire world. Along with this exploitive economic system, America also tries to control what is defined as freedom. In fact, America has the worst record of repression among all the democracies of the world.

FIGHTING FOR JUSTICE

There is something inherently evil about a country that spends more money on bombs and bullets than it does on education. All the money spent trying to bring "freedom" to Iraq with American weapons of mass destruction in just a few years could have paid for a college education at Harvard for nearly 3,000,000 students at today's tuition rates.

It is ironic how there is always money for bombs and bullets, but the penny pinching is only reserved for health care, education and other social programs. This moronic obsession with enemies keeps nearly 60,000,000 Americans mired in poverty with little hope for a decent education, adequate housing, health care or a good paying job.

America has more people incarcerated than any other country in the world. Its solution to crime is not the benevolent hand of compassion as preached by the beloved Jesus they are supposed to so dearly revere, but rather, crime is addressed by vindicate wrath and punishment, as displayed by God in the Old Testament. People must be punished, not rehabilitated.

The USA has a storied history of repressing individuals and groups that dare attempt the institution of a caring system based on social justice and economic fairness. Paradoxically, the country that talks most about freedom, particularly freedom of speech, has the most draconian laws of all the democracies in the world when it comes to people exercising the freedom of speech that is guaranteed in the Constitution that was drafted by slaveholding hypocrites in 1776.

FIGHTING FOR JUSTICE

When I was in the U.S. Army in the late 1960's and early 1970's, as this warmongering nation was engaged in an attempt to bring its corporate dominated definition of freedom to the peasants of Vietnam, who were being exploited by capitalistic masters of corruption, I first had my eyes opened to the true nature of a country that is built on a foundation of lies and deceit.

I hated that war for killing, maiming and mentally destroying so many of my friends. Yet, I am also thankful for it, as it was the one thing that opened my eyes to the barbaric hypocrisy practiced by the country I loved. Being exposed to top-secret information in the Pentagon, I learned the truth about America's suppression of freedom all over the world.

Shocked by what I learned about American attempts to install compliant governments in countries throughout the world, I began to see the real purpose of American foreign policy was the promulgation of corporate, capitalistic exploitation. Even as I write this, I am fearful that the CIA might be lurking somewhere trying to whisk me back to America to stand trial (if I would even get one) for mentioning what I have stated here. America is a nation infiltrated by evil, underhanded anti-bodies that want to spread the disease of fear throughout the populace to keep everyone in line. Stand up to the American government or defy it, and you may well find yourself locked away in the dark dungeons of one of its corporate run prisons or in one of its gulags of torture. What little freedom is left in America will not fall because of someone plotting in a cave somewhere in a Third World cesspool. The freedom will be destroyed by government leaders and the executives in the boardrooms of America who wave the flag and shout patriotic babble that the masses gobble up and digest without realizing that they are being fed a poison that will destroy freedom and make them all slaves to the corporate, governmental elite who are playing them like a fined tuned Stradivarius. Yet, like those at Jonestown, the people dutifully line up to take their Kool-Aid.

This book will lay bare the false notion of freedom in this land of hypocrisy by exploring some examples of little-known individuals who have fought lonely battles against the hypocritical establishment that wants to force all people to march in lock step to the oppressive forces that want to homogenize Americans into acceptable patterns of behaviour. Thanks to thousands of unsung, unheralded heroes who have fought lonely battles against this monolith of control, the forces of oppression have been kept at bay, but the tyrants of conformity continue to use fear as a weapon to manipulate the masses. America's leaders are always keeping the people on edge by proclaiming that others want to destroy the so-called American freedom. Truthfully, those who are destroying America's freedom are not foreigners, but rather, they are the corporate barons of greed, the religious right wing Nazis and the fascist politicians who have conditioned the American people to respond like robots to flag-waving, patriotic, religious demagoguery.

America hypocritically proclaims itself a bastion of righteousness while pointing the finger of condemnation at organizations, individuals and countries it defines as evil. Al Qaeda comes out for particular condemnation, but today and in the past, America has often supported terrorists when it was in its interests. The country that sells more armaments than any other is not North Korea, not Iran, or any other of the countries constantly referred to by American leaders as supporters of terrorist organizations. The country that sells more weapons than any other is the United States of America. In some cases, these weapons are outright gifts paid for by the American taxpayers who provide lavish corporate welfare to the defence industries that use the American treasury like it was their personal petty cash. These weapons are utilized as instruments of American foreign policy with no thought given to the fact that they are often used to keep despots in power. It is ironic that most of the weapons employed to kill Americans in Afghanistan and Iraq were originally supplied by the United States.

Throughout history, the United States has supplied terrorists in other countries with weapons, but it has also given authorities in America legal weapons to subvert, imprison and discredit those deemed a threat to the state. America has consistently made it a point to stifle those who want to question authority by locking them up or hounding them into obscurity.

FIGHTING FOR JUSTICE

CHAPTER 1
THE KING OF SWING

An editor once told me that a book without sex is a book that will not sell. Even though I am a staunch socialist, I, like so many others, occasionally am infected with that dreaded virus called greed; therefore, my first chapter will deal with sex in order to hook the reader and hopefully create a desire to explore what else I have to say. Obviously, the ultimate goal is to sell more books and increase the size of my bank account.

Elbert Poppell is a man who has been called a pervert, a purveyor of filth and a representative of the devil. Poppell is a man who has fought all his life for sexual freedom in a society that wants to suppress sexuality like it squelches other freedoms. He has been arrested, imprisoned and set-up by the police in a concentrated attempt to force conformity to a set of values based on hypocrisy. He has been vilified by politicians and ministers of mayhem who pour out a steady stream of vicious venom in attempts to control and manipulate the American populace.

Poppell comes from a humble background, as he was born on a farm in Florida around 1932. Yet, from an early age, he was a person who always questioned authority. Seeing combat in Korea during the Korean War, he was suspicious of the military's insistence on blind obedience to superiors. Never willing to discuss what he saw and did in Korea, one can only surmise that his young, inquiring mind saw through the fallacy of unquestioning obsequiousness.

FIGHTING FOR JUSTICE

He married, had a family and settled down to a life as a butcher. While better-known defenders of sexual freedom like Hugh Hefner and Larry Flynt were making headlines, Poppell was quietly building a reputation for providing places where people could openly explore their sexuality. Obviously, being young and horny made him explore the lifestyle of what was then called wife swapping with an intense vigour that was probably more rooted in the exploration of personal pleasure than noble cause. However, as government officials continued to persecute, bully and prosecute him and other practitioners, he started to see the fallacy of a society that proclaims it is the freest in the world, but has the moral police out harassing citizens who are engaging in acts the guardians of virtue deem immoral.

Obviously, in a truly democratic and free society, what consenting adults do in private should not be the business of government, the church, the mosque, the synagogue or any other organization. Poppell is a man who saw through the hypocrisy of so-called American freedom, and set out to make it his life's ambition to battle the forces of oppression that want everyone to conform to a moral code defined by a society that spends more money on weapons than education, accepts vast pockets of poverty while providing tax cuts to the wealthy, refuses health care to millions of poor people and turns a blind eye to a system of injustice based on economics and skin colour.

Fighting a constant battle with authorities throughout Florida, Poppell was eventually forced to leave the state as he was branded a purveyor of immorality by officials, who, no doubt, just like the hypocritical Republicans who pointed the finger of condemnation at Bill Clinton, were practicing deceit with the public and engaging in even more heinous acts than those of which they were accusing Poppell.

A few years in Mexico led to a more profound awaking of his sense of justice and fair play. Although America has the greatest poverty in the industrialized world, it does not compare to Mexico on the scale of economic injustice; however, since the Reagan tax cuts of the 1980's and the Bush tax give-aways to the wealthy of 2001, the gap between the rich and the poor is now even greater than it was during the Great Depression. It often seems the Republicans are hell bent on making America a Third World country where economic servitude is the norm for a populace whose only purpose is to serve the interests of the wealthy and powerful.

Poppell, was saddened by the poverty around him, and decided to return to the USA. Assuming that California was much more liberal than Florida, he packed his belongings and moved to San Diego. Although California is light years ahead of most other states in its liberal attitudes, it is still part of a country that is deeply mired in "Old Time Religion" that wants to force conformity on people. And in California, one of the most conservative cities is San Diego, where Mr. Poppell decided to set up the first of his many swing clubs.

Poppell is more than just a man who wanted to bring "swinging" into the mainstream. He is a flaunter of convention and has a roguish attitude about defending the rights of those who are not part of the vast number of Americans who always go along with the crowd and never want to rock the boat.

One example of this roguish attitude can be traced to his disillusionment with mainstream religion. In America, churches are afforded special dispensation, because of their spiritual nature. They receive tax exemptions while building huge, palatial edifices to the glorification of God, who, in my opinion would be offended by those who spend money on grandiose churches, when there are hungry people who need to be fed and clothed. If there is a God, I certainly think he or she would prefer that Christians help their fellow human beings rather than build huge fortresses of intolerance that sit empty 6 days a week. Think about how many homeless people could have a roof over their heads if the churches would unlock their doors to let those made in God's image receive a little bit of that so-called Christian charity. Why not have a minister drive down to the ghetto in his BMW or Lincoln to pick up a few homeless people and show them the real meaning of Christian love? Could you imagine Robert Schuller or Pat Robertson opening up their mansions and welcoming the homeless for a meal and a good night's sleep? Yet, these are the people who are telling the rest of us what is moral and immoral.

Poppell is a man who saw the hypocrisy of this type of religion, so he decided, as a licensed minister of the Universal Life Church, to start his own church. There was just one caveat, nudity would be allowed in the sanctuary and other parts of the church. He reasoned, according to the Constitution, freedom of religion is an absolute guarantee. Personally, I have always found that part of the Constitution particularly distressing, because, apparently freedom of religion does not mean freedom from religion.

Operating openly and with an obvious intent to test the meaning of freedom in America, Poppell was harassed, arrested and imprisoned. This, to him, was a perfect example of how Americans had no real idea what freedom meant. Americans swallow a steady diet of morality that abridges the very meaning of the word democracy. In Germany, they locked up the Jews; in America, they lock up the nonconformists.

Year after year Poppell fought a lonely battle to show that those in power were intent on destroying free thought that might lead the people to actually question those in authority. To this end, he continued to operate a variety of sex clubs that were a thorn in the side of the San Diego authorities. Being careful not to allow any drug use or prostitution, the authorities constantly had to come up with nefarious means to shut him down. Yet, even while in jail, he continued to stand up for freedom and refused to bow before the arrogant, self-righteous buffoons who practiced hypocrisy of the vilest form.

Believing that those who defend America are entitled to sexual freedom, since they are dispatched to foreign lands to fight for democratic ideals, he decided that being near a large naval base and the huge Camp Pendleton Marine complex, young boys in service would take particular delight in visiting his "Social Club" for some uninhibited sexual activity. Again, being sure not to allow prostitution, he just advertised his club as an opportunity for women and open-minded couples to meet young, virile men who would just happen to be walking around the club naked. Naturally, single women were admitted free, while the boys were charged a nominal amount. In fact, he consistently charged men with military identifications a smaller fee, since he knew they were less affluent, and were also defending the very freedom they all should have been allowed to practice.

Needless to say, the authorities were enraged by this open flaunting of sexuality. According to many officials, this kind of activity would lead to San Diego becoming a Sodom and Gomorrah. Since no specific laws were broken, the officials were taken aback when the business was filled with participants every Friday and Saturday night. Being unable to close him down, the officials set out to make his life miserable. Patrons parking on the street were ticketed for things like parking too close to the curb or too far from the curb, and even though the club was in an industrial area, authorities said there were neighbours who were complaining, in spite of the fact there was only one neighbour in the immediate vicinity. Patrons were arrested for public nuisances or other nefarious charges, as cops parked outside Poppell's establishment, waiting to pounce on people while downtown crimes of a violent nature were ignored, so they could concentrate on morality rather than real crime. Paying a battery of lawyers to fight the city kept Poppell perpetually broke, but he refused to submit to oppression from the city and the hypocritical politicians who were determined to force him to submit to their definition of morality.

Refusing to bow before the self-righteous, hypocritical morons of right wing religious ideology, Poppell came out swinging. How is that for a pun? Rather than scaling back his operations, Poppell used a bus that he had previously made into an orgy palace on wheels to pick up Marines and Naval personnel near the bases and take them for free back to his club. This further infuriated the bastions of morality who wanted to impose their views on the populace. Rather than just telling people that if they did not like this activity, they did not have to attend the parties, the moral purists decided that their views should be forced on consenting adults.

Determined not to be bullied by the police department and the self-righteous politicians, Poppell filed suit against the city for violating his civil rights by harassing him and his customers. After many years of legal battles, a federal jury awarded Poppell $200,000 in damages as they saw through the veil of lies and deceit that were used in an attempt to "frame" him for a variety of offences. The police and public officials who were called to testify were found to be less than truthful by the jury. Many members of the jury were mortified that they had to find for Poppell, because they abhorred what he was doing. However, they were also disturbed by the officials and police who thought they had the right to use any means to drive a man out of business who was breaking no laws. The men and women of the jury are, along with Poppell, genuine heroes in the battle for freedom in the land of hypocrisy. It took a great deal of courage and intestinal fortitude for these men and women who lived in the community and had to face their friends and neighbours to stand up for justice.

As one might expect, the city appealed the decision, and the case continued to drag on, costing Poppell vast amounts of money, while the city and the police just wasted taxpayers' funds to go after a man, because he dared to be a nonconformist. While they threw away money trying to force their definition of morality on people, the hungry in the city's slums still went without food and the homeless still slept on the sidewalks. Think about how many meals or rooms these defenders of morality could have supplied to the poor and homeless with the millions wasted on a callous attempt to railroad a person they considered a moral degenerate.

A public figure who refused to be named was quoted as saying, "why waste money trying to stop people from doing something that is not harming anyone? These swingers are not having sex in public. They are not doing drugs on the premises; they are not causing a public disturbance. Adult sex habits and preferences are not within the purview of government. I personally think what these people are doing is abhorrent, but what gives me or anyone else in government the right to tell consenting adults how to conduct their sex lives."

Unfortunately, this official was in the minority, as most public officials saw it as their duty to dictate to adults what was immoral, while most of them made cozy deals with developers and campaign contributors. What is more immoral, allowing greedy corporate thieves to rape the environment and fleece the taxpayers, or allowing consenting adults to visit a sex club?

These politicians set themselves up as moral guardians of virtue while they plunder the local, state and national treasuries to supply their exorbitant salaries, parsimonious benefits and lavish retirement accounts. All the while, they hypocritically pass judgment on others and try to convince the acquiescent public that great harm is being promulgated by those who do not want to follow the moral standards defined by the purveyors of hate who pour out their judgmental venom from the pulpits on Sunday mornings.

These paragons of virtue thought their appeal was in the bag, when they found out that it would be heard by a federal judge who was appointed by the "God of Conservatives," Ronald Reagan. After all, no one put on the Federal Bench by the "Great Communicator" himself could possibly side with Elbert Poppell, a representative of the devil, against the guardians of morality represented by politicians, the religious paragons of virtue, the city and the San Diego Police Department.

U.S. District Judge John Rhoades, in defence of the Constitution, shocked the entire nation when he turned down the city's request for a new trial. His comment in regards to the suit was, "no doubt, a large segment of the population views the plaintiff's activities as morally reprehensible. No doubt, the community at large views the plaintiff himself as a creepy purveyor of indecency. However, if everyone's Constitutional rights are to remain secure, you have to be careful to protect the rights of those you despise."

Ironically, the jury actually awarded Mr. Poppell more money than he sought, as they not only found the city liable for a variety of offences, but also found two police officers and a city code compliance officer guilty as well.

No less a figure than noted columnist, Ann Landers, even got into the fray over the jury award, when in her syndicated column, a reader wrote to her complaining about how immoral and outrageous this jury and judge were to come out in support of this devil of sexual immorality. To her credit, Landers defended the judge and jury, stating that although she was not keen about conducting businesses in the nude, she, nonetheless, recognized how important it is to protect the rights of those with whom we disagree.

One might assume that the matter would end here; however, San Diego is a conservative city in a liberal state. Consequently, San Diego City Councilman Juan Vargas, one never to shy away from publicity, was still intent on bringing down the wrath of the moralists on Poppell, so he called a news conference to denounce the federal verdict. Vargas told a reporter from the *Los Angeles Times* that it was an outrage for the city to be forced to pay damages to a man who infests the community with nothing more than shaded prostitution and drugs.

That statement by Vargas was patently false, as Poppell had never been charged or found guilty of practicing prostitution or dealing drugs from his place of business or any other location. To the police department's credit, they did say that, in fact, while keeping his place of business under constant surveillance there had actually never been any indication of prostitution or drug use. In fact, it was well known that Poppell would bar people from his establishment if they were caught using drugs or trying to exchange money for sex.

Poppell is not a man to suffer fools lightly or to let any person, organization or political body trample on his rights under the Constitution, so he immediately filed a lawsuit against Vargas for defamation, indicating that Vargas knew his statements to be outright lies. This lawsuit was obviously on shaky ground since Vargas was a public official, but Poppell was determined to make a point, and to make the city of San Diego pay a huge price in legal costs for trampling on his rights. To Poppell, defending the Constitution was more important than money.

The city's attorney argued that if the suit were to continue to trial it would have a detrimental effect on elected officials who need to speak out on controversial issues. Superior Court Judge Anthony C. Joseph made sure Poppell's case survived its first major challenge when he refused to dismiss it and stated the following:

"The argument that draws from me the strongest reaction is the argument about how we are somehow shutting down public officials by allowing this lawsuit to go to trial, and I am going to editorialize, although it is probably questionable whether I should."

"It would seem to me that government officials would want to be careful in the way they speak, because (sic) they owe it to themselves and the people they serve to speak honestly, correctly, with force where necessary (sic) but not to slander individuals. They don't need that. They have the power of public officials."

Once again, another judge, to his credit, defended the U.S. Constitution. Vargas, as one might expect, continued to rant and rave against Poppell and his blatant disregard for human decency and morality. In fact, he went so far as to say Poppell's neighbours had complained to him about used condoms, needles and syringes being discarded on the streets, but without producing a single person who was supposed to have complained. Nor did he produce any samples of discarded syringes, needles or condoms.

Vargas is a social conservative who has been known to attack organizations that advocate for the homeless, because he feels they are encouraging "freeloaders." Furthermore, while he was busy going after a man who was, in his opinion, morally bankrupt, he ignored the deteriorating sidewalks, burned-out streetlamps and urban blight in his district. People walking dark streets in a crime invested area, individuals living in cardboard boxes, citizens without health care, backed-up sewers and other social problems paled when compared with allowing a man to operate a club where consenting adults could have sex with one another. Meanwhile, the city's gay bathhouses were not even mentioned by Vargas. Apparently, it was all right for men to meet in a public facility and have sex, but heterosexuals needed to have "big brother" look after their morality.

Ironically, the area Vargas supposedly canvassed, talking to various residents, has only one home within 500 metres of Poppell's social club. That home is across the street from Mr. Poppell's establishment. I specifically mention it, because the person who lived there was one of my childhood heroes. The resident was former world light-heavyweight champion, Archie Moore, who had built a stately mansion at the end of the street in a time when the area was not blighted and industrialized. Yet, as the space around him deteriorated and became an commercial area, true to his humble "everyman" nature, he continued to live there until his death in 1998, enjoying an occasional swim in his boxing glove shaped backyard swimming pool. Apparently, Archie Moore had a laissez faire attitude about Poppell as he was quoted by the Associated Press as saying, "I have never had any complaints about Mr. Poppell. As a matter of fact, I have never met Mr. Poppell."

After Moore's death in 1998, Poppell bought his house, and it is now one of the most elaborate swinger's clubs in America, where there is still a lot of action going on, but no one gets knocked out, and hopefully, no one gets knocked up. (Rumour has it that Poppell supplies free condoms to his customers.) Additionally, Poppell, never one to be shy about what he does, offers tours of the establishment on his website.

As a connoisseur of antiques and old musical instruments, Poppell has a reputation for offering his customers a place with elegance and style where they can leave their inhibitions at the door, but more than that, he is a man who defends each American's right to decide what is moral and immoral without the help of some hypocritical finger-pointers who want to impose their definition of morality on the entire populace. As the masthead of the New York Times proclaims, "I may disagree with what you have to say, but I will defend to the death, your right to say it."

Remember the title of this book is *Fighting for Justice in the Land of Hypocrisy*. I am not saying Mr. Poppell has had as profound an influence on freedom of speech and sexuality as Hugh Hefner or Larry Flynt, but I am saying is that he is an unsung hero who has battled against those who want to force their definition of morality on people who are doing them no harm, and are causing no caustic mischief in a society that sanctions the greatest evil known to mankind, the evil of poverty, injustice and imperialistic military subjugation of the entire world to corporate thievery and exploitation.

In graduate school, one of the most interesting courses I took was *American Freedom and Ethics*. I had a wonderful professor who opened my eyes to the hypocrisy of a country that constantly talked about freedom, but then did all it could to suppress that freedom by allowing religion to dictate public moral policy. He was very quick to point out that it was religion that led to people being put in stocks, so-called witches being burned at the stake, capital punishment being carried out in the name of justice and even segregation being approved by states because the Bible sanctioned it.

In one of the course books, I was particularly appalled in regards to Idaho laws on morality. For many years, the state banned anything but the missionary position for fornication. In one particular case, a peeping tom was watching through a bedroom window, when a man and woman were having sex. When he saw them reverse position and perform oral sex on one another, he reported them to authorities, who promptly prosecuted the couple for breaking Idaho's fornication law. Paradoxically, the peeping tom was never prosecuted for his crime.

As recently as 1998, a gay couple was prosecuted in Georgia when police raided their apartment and found them having anal sex, which was still illegal under Georgia law; although, that law has subsequently been changed, much to the chagrin of Republican legislators and Christian fundamentalists.

So, what Poppell has done is simply refuse to bend before the wind of oppression blown by those who think they have the right definition of morality. I am particularly distressed by those public officials who proclaim fealty to a thick black book called the Bible that sanctions slavery, death for adulterers, selling daughters to the highest bidders, polygamy and a variety of other acts. Thanks to people like Elbert

FIGHTING FOR JUSTICE

Poppell, the San Diego moral guardians of hypocrisy know that they will pay a high price if they try to abridge the people's right to think for themselves.

American school children read about presidents and politicians in America's sanitized history books. These books will not mention people who have "rocked the boat" and refused to bend to the machinations of the moral guardians of virtue who want to interfere with the people's freedom of thought, choice and deed. Like the Taliban, these misguided, self-righteous hypocrites want to impose their definition of morality on the populace.

Fortunately, there have been a few individuals who have stood tall against those who would put all Americans under the feet of jacked-booted moral hypocrites who think they have the right to impose their attitudes and views on those who prefer to think for themselves. Most Americans lack the moral courage to battle against these barons of banality. Those who genuinely love freedom should be thankful for people like Elbert Poppell, who always refused to bend before the self-righteous moral hypocrites who fear a populace that might think for themselves.

Elbert Poppell's name will never appear in American history books, but it belongs right beside other American heroes who have defended the people's right to freedom of thought. He, and those like him are true American icons, dedicated to battling against those who would imprison all of the country to their narrow-minded, hypocritical definition of morality. LONG LIVE THE KING OF SWING.

CHAPTER 2
FREEDOM OF PRESS:
IGNORANCE FOR THE MASSES

In the previous chapter, we saw how one man could make a difference when it comes to defending freedom. However, most Americans have no idea what the real meaning of freedom is. They swallow a steady diet of propaganda that convinces them their country is superior to all others when it comes to freedom. Freedom of speech was the very first Amendment in the U.S. Constitution, because it was considered the most important. Yet, most Americans do not realize that of all the so-called democracies in the world, the USA ranks near the bottom when it comes to freedom of speech. Each year, the United Nations ranks the countries of the world in variety of areas based on a specific formula. One of those areas is freedom of speech, which includes freedom of the press. In order to be well informed, citizens must have access to information that is uncensored and allowed to circulate freely. The below chart illustrates where America stands according to the Freedom of Press International Index.

Freedom of Press Index
(Note: Index is based on 0 being the best and 50 being the worst)

1. Finland
2. Norway
3. Estonia
4. Netherlands
5. Austria
6. Iceland

7. Switzerland
8. Cape Verde
9. Denmark
10. Canada
47. United States

The above chart rates the USA 47th in press freedom, according to the United Nations. Knowing how most Americans are propagandized into believing the U.N. is anti-American, perhaps we should look at one other survey, so that those who question the United Nations have a different reference source. Another group (*Reporters without Borders*) made up of reporters from all over the democratic world also rates freedom of press in 179 countries. They place the USA at number 57 in the world.

One might note that countries like Canada, Sweden and Belgium rank slightly lower in the *Reporters without Borders* rankings, because they have stringent laws against "hate speech." The author of this book deplores hate speech. Yet, I think freedom of speech should never be abridged regardless of how vile it might be, which means no matter how disgusting the idea promulgated from the lips of a speaker, the right to speak should be inviolate and absolute.

Let us look at a few examples of how America has traditionally tried to abridge freedom of press and speech when it is used to attack the status quo. All who question authority in America are considered subversive. People are brought up from an early age to worship at the altar of patriotic servitude that instils the idea of American superiority.

FIGHTING FOR JUSTICE

After two and one-half years in the U.S. Army toward the end of the Vietnam War, I returned to North Carolina to seek public office. At the age of 25, I just qualified age-wise to run for the House of Representatives. Being a Democrat in a highly Republican district, I did not stand a very good chance of winning the election. However, after winning the Democratic primary election handily, I did come within 290 votes of being elected in the general election.

For many years, I sort of blamed my father for losing the election, as he offered no financial assistance in my run for the office, or any real moral support after we had a brief conversation about my plans for the campaign. He took one look at my campaign biography and said, "son, you have down here that you have a Ph.D. You are running in a district full of working people. Get that Ph.D. off your biography, because they will think you look down on working people, even though, you and I know that is not true. Then, you need to visit the barbershop and get that shoulder length long hair cut, because they would never vote for a person who looks like a dope-smoking, communist hippie."

I was irate that my father would suggest that I compromise my principles to win the election. I told him that I would not be a hypocrite just to represent the people. What the people saw is what the people would get. The length of my hair or the casual clothes I wore had nothing to do with the kind of person I was. I even went so far as to remind him that Jesus wore sandals, long hair and a flowing robe.

FIGHTING FOR JUSTICE

In my father's indelible way, he replied, "yes and these goddamn Christian voters would also slam the church door in Jesus' face if he showed up at church looking like that today. They would not even elect him city dogcatcher, because of his long hair and scraggly beard. I am not wasting my time or money on an election you can't win, because you won't do something simple like cut your hair. You don't understand that right or wrong, your appearance has more to do with what the people think about you than your ideas do. People are stupid! Why do you think they keep electing the same jerks to office all the time? When I designed a sewing machine, I had it made in yellow, because people think it is prettier than the typical black Singer machine. It is not as good a machine as a Singer is, but it is prettier, so they buy it. When I build a house, I dress up the outside and make it as beautiful as possible, but I always build the same floor plan inside, because I know exactly what it will cost me to build and it is functional. People look at the exterior, and then they tend to overlook any flaws on the inside. You have a lot to learn. A Ph.D. doesn't necessarily make you smart. It can often make you just an educated fool."

My feelings were deeply hurt at the time, but looking back on it, I have a much better understanding today of the wisdom he was trying to share with me. I think I would still probably change the way he said what he did, but I do see the validity of what he had to say.

Most of my campaigning was at cotton mills, hosiery mills, jeans plants, furniture manufacturers and shirt plants, which were the chief industries in the district at the time. Although I always had a soft spot for the working man, until my first trip into a cotton mill, I never realized the agony and pain so many people must go through each day in order to put food on the table. As I walked around a Franklinville, North Carolina cotton mill, shaking hands and picking the flying lint out of my hair and eyes, I found the constant drone of the clacking machines almost deafening. The noise was so loud that I had to scream at each person in order to be heard. It was the early 1970's, and not a single person had any protection from the noise.

After 30 minutes in the mill, shaking hands with 400 or 500 people, I walked out to my car, opened the door, slid in, put my head down on the steering wheel and cried. I had known moderate poverty for awhile as a small child, and I knew that my mother and father worked in a cotton mill for 37 ½ cents an hour at one time, but I never knew the conditions in which they had worked in order to feed and clothe me. I was overwhelmed with a new understanding of what it was like to have to work for the barons of greed who controlled America. From that day forward, I have always had a soft spot in my heart for the real working people of the world who toil in isolated despair in a system of greed that reduces men and women to fodder in a machine that grinds them up and disposes of them when they have served their purpose.

I am sure my twelfth grade English teacher, Miss Powell, would say that in a chapter on freedom of speech and the press, I have gone astray from the topic. However, there is a method to my convoluted discourse above.

FIGHTING FOR JUSTICE

I am sure that most people wonder what running for office and visiting cotton mills has to do with freedom of speech. Ironically, it goes to the heart of freedom of speech, because when I brought up my visits to the mills with party officials, and indicated I wanted to spend more time on the issues relating to working people, their response was that they did not vote in large numbers, and that they were mostly interested in religious issues. They wanted their children to be able to pray in school and have the Ten Commandants put up on public buildings. Other than those issues, I would just be wasting time and party money on things that were unimportant. To that end, I could only receive free radio time based upon issues the party wanted to cover. If I wanted to include other issues, it was up to me to raise my own money or pay for the time myself. Having been in the army the prior 2 ½ years, as well as completing my doctoral degree, unfortunately my financial situation was untenable. So, even as a candidate for office, the political power brokers had control over what I could say. Freedom of speech exists in America only for those who can afford it. In other words, the government, corporations and the wealthy have the means to communicate their message while those without the means can bend to their will or be voices crying in the wilderness.

I once had professor who said, "freedom of speech is absolute when used in defence of the status quo. When used by the anti-establishment, it is not as absolute."

Throughout history, America has attempted to maintain control of those who would question authority. You often hear that without authority there would be no order. What that really means is, without authority, those in power might have to bend to the will of the people. Do Congress and the President represent the will of the American people as they are supposed to as spelled out in the Constitution? Or, do they represent the will of the powerful and wealthy?

Americans have been manipulated into believing they are superior to all other societies. It is, for that reason, the government can still get the poor and lower middle class youths to sign-up to defend "freedom" while the offspring of the wealthy and powerful stay at home to reap the benefits of a society that is supposed to promote equality. While the poor are dodging bullets in the next country destined for good old American style democracy, the sons and daughters of the President and members of Congress are busy dodging their responsibilities to their country.

George Bush told the public that America's youths in uniform were defending a way of life envied by those who could not understand freedom. Even Barrack Obama extolled the virtues of those who sign up to kill America's enemies. Let us look at that freedom that is so precious that America constantly sends it youth off to fight in the struggle of good verses evil.

While these youths were dying to defend this so-called freedom in Iraq and Afghanistan, a high school teacher in Indiana lost her job as editorial adviser to the school newspaper for allowing an article to appear that advocated tolerance of the gay lifestyle. Amy Sorrell was transferred to another school, where she was refused any position dealing with journalism for fear that she might allow avowed homosexuals to have a forum for their lifestyle. Of course, I am sure the School Board would have no problem if she had allowed an editorial in support of capitalism. The fact that it is a system based on greed and exploitation is not immoral like homosexuality is.

Amy Sorrell would have loved to fight the School Board over this egregious abridgment of freedom of speech, but like so many of us, she simply said that she could not financially afford to fight the authorities in court. One might logically assume this was a case that occurred many years ago, long before America became a more "enlightened society." Unfortunately, it occurred in 2007. This is an example of how those in positions of authority have the power of the establishment behind them, while those who want to fight for justice are forced to bend to oppression, because they lack financial resources in a system that is based on economics rather than fairness.

I wonder how many times I have heard people say, "in America, you can say whatever you want, because we have freedom of speech." Allen Lee of Cary, Illinois might have a different idea after his 2007 arrest for disorderly conduct.

What was his disorderly conduct? He wrote an essay in his high-school creative writing class about a deranged killer who opened fire on high school students, then had sex with the dead bodies. After the teacher turned in his essay to authorities, they decided it was disturbing and inappropriate. Here was a straight-A student who found himself under arrest for exercising the so-called freedom of speech that is bally-hoed as one of America's greatest freedoms. In the early 1800's, abolitionists wrote essays attacking slavery. I suppose these same authorities would have found those essays disturbing and inappropriate since they attacked the accepted norms of the day.

Ironically, after the arrest, it came out in a newspaper article that this "evil" boy had enlisted in the Marines to fight for the very freedoms he was being denied.

In the first chapter of the book, I covered sexual freedom rather candidly. However, I think the same topic must also be touched upon in this chapter since there has been an American tradition of trying to control sexual content in speech, writing and media. To do so, let me once again recall a bit of personal history.

In the early 1970's, a small-town country boy named Wayne Frye accepted a position with Hunter College of the City University of New York and departed North Carolina for the sinful environs of New York City. Working at the college's main campus on Park Avenue, I was only a short distance from that devil's den of inequity, Times Square. Being young and curious (not to mention, extremely virile, as most youths are), one of my early two-hour lunchtime strolls was to Times Square. I was shocked, but incredibly intrigued, by an area that freely advertised sex shops, had nude pictures of women posted outside clubs and was inundated with non-conformist sidewalk hawkers who offered everything from naked pictures to vagina-shaped popsicles. It was difficult for me to comprehend that people were allowed this much freedom, because I was from a community where we were even forced to keep our shirts tucked-in at high school, because an exposed shirt-tail was a sign of rebellious youth that would not be tolerated in a God-fearing community.

Even though I had an overwhelming desire to go into some of these dens of sin, as I stood in front of a sex shop, I hesitated and decided it would be inappropriate for a college professor, no matter how young, to be seen in such a seedy place. Did I want to go in? Of course I did. I was 25 years old and had never been into such a place, even when I was in the army. The temptation was overwhelming, but my small-town, repressed background played on my young, impressionable mind, and made me think that exposure to such evil might actually lead me to perdition. The years of exposure to ministers and community leaders who preached against the evils of sex, and how exposure to pornography would turn even the best of people into graven sex maniacs, made me turn my back on these evils and head back to work a bit despondent over not having the courage to at least take a little peek into those "adult stores."

Upon returning to the campus, a student, sitting on the floor, reading a thick tabloid newspaper, was waiting outside my office. As I looked at the back of the paper, I saw that it had obvious sexual content. Unashamed, the student got up, went into my office and discussed a problem he was having with an assignment I had given. Upon leaving, he left the newspaper behind. Desperately wanting to read it,

O.K., look at it, I slipped it in my briefcase, for fear that my colleagues might see me with it, and I took it home.

I had never bought a *Playboy* or any other sexually-oriented magazine. Notice, that I did not say I had never looked at any, only that I never spent any money on them. Anyway, as I opened my briefcase and spread the paper out on the kitchen table, I was in disbelief when I refolded it so I could start with page one. In huge letters at the top of the page was the publications name, *Screw Magazine*.

Al Goldstein was born in 1936 in New York City, and for years, he fondly referred to himself as a Jewish-American publisher and pornographer. He was the brains behind the most irreverent, outlandish, establishment-bashing magazine ever published, *Screw Magazine*. It was more than just a sex publication that included ads for prostitutes, masseurs and masseuses, swingers, sex shops and quality papers to use for rolling pot; it was an iconic, free willing magazine that poked fun at the hypocrisy of an establishment that wanted to control and manipulate people.

Parlaying a $150 investment in 1968 into a multimillion-dollar empire in only a few short years, Goldstein was on the moralistic hypocrites' hit list from the very beginning. He was a person who threatened the moral fabric of a society that sanctioned greed as a virtue in an unbalanced economic system, tolerated poverty in order to satisfy the need for cheap labour, allowed children to go without healthcare and squandered billions on building weapons of mass destruction while ignoring its own people's basic needs. All these things paled when compared to allowing an immoral panderer to distribute a publication that showed people having sex, parodied politicians, attacked sexual hypocrisy and laid bare (how is that for a pun) the real lack of press freedom in a nation that constantly proclaimed itself to be the bastion of democracy. Al Goldstein became a target of the moral defenders of virtue who saw evil in every penis and bare breast that graced the pages of *Screw Magazine*.

Knowing that there were more votes from the Christian right than from the liberal left, politicians fell in line and got on the anti-Goldstein bandwagon. Constant harassment from authorities kept Goldstein's lawyers busy defending him from a variety of charges aimed at stopping the presses from rolling out a steady stream of anti-establishment, pornographic literature and pictures. All this animosity aimed at a publication that had a top circulation of only 530,000 in the late 1970's.

Politicians soon learned that attacking Al Goldstein and trying to abridge his free speech rights was tantamount to placing a bull's eye on their chests. Richard Nixon, several attorneys general and a variety of religious figures came in for special criticism on the pages of *Screw*.

I read the magazine only one time and even with my liberal attitudes found it disgusting. I never again picked up a copy, but I do applaud Goldstein for his commitment to freedom of the press. The masthead of the *New York Times* says, "I may disagree with what you have to say, but I will defend your right to say it." I feel about Screw Magazine that way. I find it offensive and distasteful, but Mr. Goldstein had a right to publish it, just as I have the right to askew buying it.

It is ironic that pornographers seem to be at the very fore-front of protecting America's First Amendment rights that have never been fully implemented in a society that at one time considered the paintings of the Italian masters pornographic, because they often portrayed women and men frolicking about naked. Of course, what could you expect from a country that as recently as 2002 had an Attorney General (John Ashcroft) who had statues in the Justice Department covered with white tarp, because they showed women's breasts. People like this would probably like to see doctors' come up with a method of clothing baby's in the womb, so their genitals would not be exposed when they are born.

It is my intention to concentrate on the unsung heroes who have not made an inordinate number of headlines over the years in their battles against the forces of oppression, but it is difficult to exclude from a chapter on freedom of the press one man who has been paramount in attacking the hypocritical moralists who run America. He is a man labelled the "King of Sleaze," "The Truck-Drivers' Pornographer," and the "Redneck Playboy Emulator." Larry Flynt is much more than that.

I must admit that I have never bought a *Hustler* magazine. However, that does not mean that I have never seen one. I am notorious for being cheap and the one thing I never spent money on were sex magazines; although, I certainly have looked at many that were in the possession of friends, and a few I found in the possession of my youngest son when he was a teenager. I confiscated them from him only briefly, then when his mother was satisfied that I had done my moral duty, I clandestinely gave them back to him.

It is estimated that the average *Playboy* magazine has a pass-on circulation of four for every one sold. I am sure that with a lower socio-economic target market, *Hustler's* pass on circulation is much higher.

Larry Flynt, like so many Americans, was born into a poverty-stricken household in 1942. His sister, who died from leukemia at the age of four, is rumoured to have had no access to competent medical care in a country that has always made it a privilege rather than a right. Upon her death, Larry, at the age of ten, left Kentucky to live with his grandparents in Indiana. Like so many poor youths, he saw the military as a way out of poverty and enlisted in the U.S. Navy at the age of fifteen. He eventually served on the *U.S.S. Enterprise*.

Having been in a psychiatric institution for a brief time after leaving the Navy, upon his release, Flynt purchased a Cincinnati bar in a run down part of town that he turned into a working-class strip club. He opened up several other "Hustler Clubs" in Ohio, and became a thorn in the side of politicians and the moral leaders of the community who saw him as an abomination.

FIGHTING FOR JUSTICE

It was also about this time that he met Althea Leisure, an underage stripper, who had recently left an orphanage where she was reared after her father killed her mother and grandparents before committing suicide. She became Flynt's sexual and business partner. Offended by what he saw as an elitist attitude on the part of *Penthouse* and *Playboy* magazines, he surmised that the working-class deserved their own magazine that was more real and down-to-earth.

The first edition came out in 1974, and Flynt, disappointed with the initial editions, eventually hired *Screw* magazine's Bruce David to make *Hustler* just as irreverent as *Screw*. It was Larry Flynt who was the first mainstream sex magazine publisher to dare to show the spread vagina. Unlike *Playboy* and *Penthouse*, Flynt did not airbrush his models and made it a point to feature graphic sexual photos of disabled, pregnant, elderly and obese women. His magazine proudly displayed the real women of America, not the *Playboy* airbrushed mannequins.

He reached his peak of irreverence with the publication of photos of Jackie Kennedy Onassis cavorting about nude on a Greek island. The paragons of virtue ranted and raved against this affront to the former first lady, while ignoring the fact that if a person is going nude where they can be seen, they must not be too concerned about being photographed.

Flynt compiled a long list of arrests on charges of pandering and obscenity, but continued, unabated, to defend his rights under the First Amendment. Economics was, no doubt, the primary factor in his rabid defence of his rights, as he wanted to protect his considerable income; however, the residual effect was the protection of every American's First Amendment rights.

Flynt tried to prove his point about obscenity by publishing a pamphlet showing the atrocities of war and asking which was worse, the carnage of war or a naked woman. This reminds me of the time I was in the army during the Vietnam War, and the Pentagon brass had a fit, because some of the soldiers wrote, "Fuck Ho Chi Minh" on the bombs that were being dropped on the women and children of North Vietnam. Dropping bombs on women and children was not an obscenity, but writing, "Fuck Ho Chi Minh" was? This is the kind of convoluted thinking that has made America the most hypocritical nation on earth.

Although many people found the images of war offensive, Flynt proved his point by showing that images of war could be sent through the mail without censorship, while photos of people having sex were considered obscene. His many obscenity convictions in lower courts were ultimately overturned on appeal.

In 1977, he met a woman named Ruth Carter Stapleton, who was the evangelist sister of President Jimmy Carter. Saying that she and Flynt shared many of the same ideas on sex, they became friends. On an airplane trip with Stapleton, he experienced a vision from God, and became a born-again Christian. He vowed to make Hustler a Christian magazine. This was the same time that his wife, Althea, said, "the Lord may have entered Larry's life, but $20,000,000 a year has just left his life." Fortunately, this sudden conversion did not alter his stand on protecting American's First Amendment rights. However, that dedication would eventually cost him dearly.

In 1978, he was charged with obscenity in the small Georgia town of Lawrenceville. The guardians of morality are particularly strong in Georgia, and one of them was about to rain down the wrath of God on this perverted, anti-Christian, blasphemous sinner.

One day when he left court, a representative of America's outraged moralists, shot him. Though not killed, he would be confined to a wheelchair for the rest of his life. It was at that time that he was quoted as saying, "if those Christians would take a good dose of lithium, they would be just fine, and the chances are that all those visions would go away."

Becoming addicted to painkillers did not deter him from continuing his fight for justice. His many court appearances continued unabated, and his behaviour became more outrageous as the so-called justice system continued its attempts to silence him and his publications. He shouted profanities in the courtroom, and even went so far as to wear an American flag as a diaper in court, proclaiming, "if they're going to treat me like a baby, I'm going to act like one."

When Flynt parodied Jerry Falwell's hypocrisy with a sexually suggestive cartoon in *Hustler*, Falwell filed suit against him for libel and intent to inflict emotional distress. The jury found Flynt not guilty of libel, but even though he clearly placed the phrase "intended as a parody" at the bottom of the cartoon, the jury did find him guilty of intent to inflict emotional distress and awarded the Reverend Falwell 200,000 U.S. dollars in compensation. Flynt, refusing to bow before the sanctimonious righteousness of the right wing religious bigots, appealed the decision all the way to the Supreme Court, where the court overturned the verdict.

Amazingly, no less a conservative jurist than William Rehnquist, appointed to the Supreme Court by that bastion of the right wing Richard Nixon and then nominated as Chief Justice by Mr. Conservative, himself, Ronald Reagan, ruled in favour of Flynt, stating that any reasonable person would know that the cartoon was obviously a parody. Despite a history of voting a strictly conservative line on most cases, he concluded the verdict with a terse statement that reinforced the sanctity of the First Amendment, "at the heart of the First Amendment is the recognition of the fundamental importance of the free flow of ideas and opinions on matters of public interest and concern."

Flynt was equally eloquent after the decision, stating, "we have to tolerate things that we may not like, so we can be free. Free press is not just freedom for the thought you love, but for the thought you hate."

This landmark decision made it possible to criticize public figures without the criticizer being liable for suit under the emotional distress doctrine. Without people like Larry Flynt, who, fortunately, had the financial resources to pursue this case, all Americans would have suffered one more blow to their already diminishing freedoms. Had an average person been sued by Falwell, with his vast resources culled from his "flock" that flooded him with donations for his estate and high living, the verdict might have stood, because most people would not have the financial resources to fight a powerful man like Falwell.

During the impeachment trial of Bill Clinton for his White House "blow job," Flynt publications exposed several Republican Congressmen who were also guilty of adultery. This led to many of them scurrying to cover their tracks because of the hypocrisy they exhibited in condemning Clinton for the same thing they were doing. They defended themselves by saying they did not lie before a Grand Jury about it, as if any sane man would freely admit to his wife that he was having sex with another woman.

Ironically, a few years later, when these same hypocritical Republicans learned about George Bush's lies in regards to Iraqi weapons of mass destruction, they had no interest in impeaching him for lying. My question to them would be how many lives did Bill Clinton's lie cost? The number of American service men killed due to Bush's lies is around 5,000. Which is a greater breech of morality – lying about a "blow job" that caused no deaths, or lying about weapons of mass destruction that led to over 5000 American deaths and between 200,000 to 500,000 Iraqi deaths?

It is rumoured that Bill Clinton even continued to conduct business over the phone while Monica was on her knees doing that for which she became famous. To me, that is truly a man dedicated to serving the people. He continued to conduct the people's business even while he was seeking sexual gratification. Can anyone imagine Bush even having sex, much less conducting the people's business while doing it? This is a man whom you can easily imagine not being able to chew gum and walk at the same time. Do not take this as a rousing endorsement of Bill Clinton, because as you will see in later chapters, I have not always been thrilled with his policies, either. This is merely an attack on hypocrisy.

The recent American hysteria over terrorism is a good example of how those in power want to exercise maximum control of the populace. I wonder how many times I have had friends in the USA talk about "sleeper cells." This is just another example of the American government's use of scare tactics to keep the public on edge. Any reasonably intelligent person should know that if Al Qaeda were able to strike again they would have done so. It would be so easy to place bombs in shopping centres, ferries, buses, on bridges, buildings in small towns and various other public facilities. Yet, the American people actually believe that their government has prevented this from occurring. With illegal immigrants flocking across the Mexican border daily to supply American capitalists with cheap labour, it would take no real effort for Al Qaeda operatives to infiltrate America and complete countless acts of terrorism. Yet, they have not done so, not because of the American government's diligence, but because it simply does not have the ability to do so. Al Qaeda is more of a manufactured threat than a real one. They were not even in Iraq until the "Boob from Texas" decided to prove that he was a man by using innocent women and children for targets as he bombed Iraqi cities into rubble, so the big construction corporations could make billions rebuilding what "Two Gun Bush" destroyed. Of course, the big corporations that made the bombs were also delighted to watch the supplies of weapons depleted, so they could make billions re-supplying the military with the weapons the USA wants to deny others, but freely uses itself to subjugate millions to the will of corporate America.

In today's repressed American environment, the above paragraph alone might lead to a knock on my door by the FBI, if I were still in the USA. The paranoia of the American thought police actually emulates the Taliban, whom they tell the American public are the extreme example of evil.

As a young man, I was even more outspoken about corporate malfeasance and government suppression than I am today. For that reason, I assumed that I would have to pursue a career in academia, because freedom of speech is also supposed to extend to those who teach in America's colleges and universities, and to a much lesser degree (based upon history) to secondary and elementary teachers. Historically, this has been a right consistently abridged by a government that wants to maintain the status quo and teach people not to question authority.

In 1972, as the youngest professor at Hunter College of the City University of New York, I was blessed to have a Department Chairperson who strongly believed in "freedom of speech" for his faculty. Therefore, when some in power tried to abridge my freedom of speech, Fulton Ross stood by me and insisted that I was a person who offered students an open and intellectually engaging classroom; therefore, I had his complete confidence and support. Ironically, over 30 years later, at the end of my career, things had not really changed, as authorities still wanted a compliant staff that would train students not to question authority. My supervisor in the Los Angeles School District, where I was Director of an Intensive Academic Support program for at risk youth is an example of someone who stood up for freedom of speech. When authorities tried to stifle my freedom of speech, she simply told those who were more interested in teaching discipline and compliance with a set of rules than teaching free thought, that the best thing they could do was leave a man who was doing a good job alone. To her credit, she always saw that the staff, my students and I received the support we needed. Unfortunately, this kind of individual is a rarity in today's academic world, which is now like a corporation that requires obedient employees who will toe the corporate line. Like corporate executives, administrators receive excessive compensation, while the real workers (teachers) are considered mere employees, whose job is to train and prepare their students to grow into employees to serve the master corporation.

Having tenure can assure one that it will be difficult be fired, but it does not preclude a person from being transferred to one school after another, or from being harassed by administrators. Fortunately, I was always lucky to have administrators who stood by me and defended academic freedom. Even when I was at a religious affiliated university in California, my dear friend, the Dean of the School of Business, made it clear that I was free to teach my way, even if I was at a religiously affiliated university. However, there are many colleges, universities and school districts where those in authority want to be sure that students are programmed to think in a certain way. Does anyone really believe that there is complete academic freedom of speech at a school like Liberty University that was founded by Jerry Falwell and his Christian right-wing flag wavers? What about Oral Roberts University? I wonder how many atheists they have on their staff? How can a university truly educate people when it refuses to open up the classroom to varied opinions and ideas?

One of the recent example of attempts by authorities to abridge the right of academic freedom of speech involves a Chicago professor. As an outspoken supporter of Palestinian rights, Norman Finkelstein was the target of those who wanted to make sure students in America's colleges only get one side of a story when it comes to supporting the USA and its allies.

A well-known scholar with a Ph.D. in Political Science from Princeton University, Professor Finkelstein spent most of his academic career in the wasteland of adjunct professorships at schools that want to utilize cheap labour to maximize their cash flow, so they can devote more resources to bloated administrative salaries and benefits. By using adjunct faculty, and paying only a few thousand dollars per course, they avoid hiring full-time teachers who would command from $60,000 to well over $100,000 per year.

FIGHTING FOR JUSTICE

For many years, in spite of his reputation for excellent teaching and scholarship, he wondered from one university to another in search of that elusive job that might finally lead to a tenure-track position. He assumed he had found one when he accepted a full-time position at DePaul University in 2002. He attributes many of his problems with securing a regular position to his doctoral dissertation, which attacked Zionism. Jobs are often contingent on a letter of recommendation from the dissertation committee. His committee refused to supply him with one, in spite of the fact that they accepted his dissertation and approved the awarding of a doctoral degree. Did his subject have something to do with this refusal?

He has been accused of anti-Semitism, despite that fact that he is Jewish and his mother and father are survivors of the Warsaw ghetto and German concentration camps. In his book *The Holocaust Industry, Reflections on the Exploitation of Jewish Suffering*, he attacks the Jewish organizations that attempt to extort money from European countries for collusion with the Nazis during World War II. He particularly abhors the obscene salaries drawn by the heads of these organizations while the victims of the death camps receive minuscule settlements. He quotes an authoritative source that indicated some consultants are paid up to $700 per hour for their work, with some bringing in excess of a million dollars a year, all on the backs of the victims who are the ones who should be receiving fair compensation.

Nowhere in his work does he make any excuses for Nazi barbarism. However, he does lay bare the part the

German capitalists played in bringing Hitler to power and their profiteering from the prolific war machine that kept German industry humming along for so many years.

He says Germany has been extorted enough, both financially and morally, for its ill deeds almost 70 years ago, as has Switzerland, which served as the Nazis bank. He also says that the over $60 billion dollars Germany has paid is not going to benefit the dwindling number of survivors who are still alive, but rather enrich those who have made a cottage industry out of the Holocaust. Contempt for the Germany of the 20's, 30's and 40's should not equate to transferring that hate to modern Germans who are divorced from the Nazi past, according to Finkelstein.

However, he really puts the nail in the coffin, when he says the USA never compensated Jews who tried to flee the Nazis and were turned back when they arrived in America. Many of these people would later die in concentration camps. American banks also accepted transferable Jewish assets from Europe, but after the end of the war, there was no attempt by them to locate the heirs of those who had died in the camps while their assets were being used by American banks. He then goes further to ask why the USA supports compensation for the Jews, but itself, denies that it owes any compensation to African-Americans for enslaving their ancestors, which is one of the root causes for the descendants who live in poverty and for years were denied the most basic of human rights that were enjoyed by the white majority. And what about Native Americans?

FIGHTING FOR JUSTICE

All this leads to the concentrated campaign by outside individuals and organizations that urged the university to deny him tenure, because of his public opposition to Israeli policies in the occupied territories. More precisely, the powerful in America do not want to reward those who step out of line when it comes to public policy. Is he a poor teacher? There is no proof of that whatsoever. Is he not a published writer? Numerous books and articles attest to his abilities as an accomplished scholar. The Political Science Department and the personnel committee of the College of Liberal Arts and Sciences supported him for tenure. However, the Dean refused to endorse his candidacy for tenure. Of course, the department and the college committee are made up of Finkelstein's peers, and, no doubt, one high-paid individual administrator's opinion will always trump the opinion of the ordinary workers.

I cannot conclude the discussion of free speech without also including one of my favourite examples of free-speech suppression from the 1960's, an era when many Americans were actually demanding an end to the capitalistic exploitation of the people and the institution of a genuinely democratic and equalitarian system of government.

As an example of the superficiality of the American public, Angela Davis is remembered today more for her wild Afro hairdo than for her commitment to social justice. Angela was born in 1944 in the heart of segregationist America, Birmingham, Alabama. Her father gave-up a teaching job to run a service station, because the black teachers were paid so poorly.

Spending time with New York relatives, she was exposed to integration at an early age, but upon returning to Alabama, she suffered the degradation and humiliation of institutionalized segregation. Although she went to sub-standard, dilapidated, poor black schools, her intellect led to a high-school scholarship at a New York City private school, where she became acquainted with socialism and was friends with the children whose parents were members of the America Communist Party.

She attended undergraduate school in the United States, but went to Europe for graduate work, where she earned a Ph.D. in Philosophy at Humboldt University in Berlin, Germany. Her academic sojourn in Europe exposed her to more equalitarian and just societies where segregation was not tolerated or practiced. She was convinced that the hopes of African-Americans lay in a rejection of the capitalistic domination promulgated on the working class by the wealthy barons of greed.

Her scholarship and intellect led to a job as one of the youngest Assistant Professors at UCLA in 1969. Her membership in the Communist Party did not prevent the Philosophy Department from hiring someone they saw as a promising teacher and scholar. However, it just so happens that a towering symbol of right-wing righteousness and flag-waving patriotism was California's governor at the time. Ronald "Destroy the Evil Empire" Reagan was appalled that a state institution would allow enough freedom of speech to permit a known member of the Communist Party to teach impressionable undergraduates who might actually learn to question the capitalistic domination of the working classes.

Reagan squealed like a stuffed pig before Joseph McCarthy's Senate Committee on Un-American Activities in 1951, naming many of the Hollywood elite that he had called friends as either communists or communist sympathizers, in the process, leading to them being blacklisted and their careers being destroyed. While he was appearing in ads telling consumers that Chesterfield cigarettes were good for your health, he was appalled at the lies he said the communists were promulgating on the American people. This moral guardian of virtues could not tolerate a known communist being a member of the UCLA faculty, and he insisted that every teacher should sign an oath attesting that they were not now or had they ever been a member of the communist party. At Reagan's behest, the Board of Regents of the University of California fired her in 1969. She was later rehired after a community uproar over this blatant inference in academic freedom perpetrated by Reagan. Meanwhile, "Mr. Communicator," went on to greater fame and glory as President of the USA, destroying the unions and awarding the rich huge tax breaks, which was far less evil than belonging to the Communist Party that wanted to let the working man get his fair share of the American dream that has traditionally only been the province of the rich and powerful.

Davis went on to greater fame and glory herself. She made the FBI's Ten Most Wanted List (only the third woman to appear on the list at the time) after she was implicated in the daring escape of William Christmas, who was on trail in a non-lethal stabbing incident. Christmas and an accomplice (Jonathan Jackson) kidnapped the judge and members of the jury, demanding on their way out of the courthouse that three members of the Black Panther Party who were in Soledad Prison be freed if the judge was to live. An overly zealous police reaction led to a wild shootout that resulted in the deaths of Christmas, Jackson and the judge.

What does this have to do with Angela Davis? The government had been after her for a long time because of her known communist leanings and her work with the Black Panther Party. Supposedly, this bright, highly intelligent, well-known public personality had actually gone out and bought the guns used in this escape attempt. The FBI, long known for its circumvention of the Constitution in pursuit of communists and Black Panthers, decided this would be a way to get this "uppity black woman" and put her safely behind bars where they had put so many other radicals who dared challenge the American system of corporate slavery and racist intimidation.

Expecting to be railroaded by the forces of repression, Davis went on the run for two months, before being caught in New York City. While incarcerated at the New York City Women's Detention Centre, she organized prisoners and helped set up a bail program for those who could not afford to post bonds. She was once again appalled by a country where the wealthy can post bail while awaiting trial, but the poor had to spend weeks, months and even years in jail while awaiting trail, because they did not have the financial resources to post bail. The penal authorities were not too happy with her time in prison, as it just gave her another opportunity to highlight the inequity of the American system of justice where the wealthy receive a slap on the wrist and a fine, while the poor are carted off to the slammer.

Her trial was a showcase for radical thought as the American system of justice itself was actually put on trial. To the amazement of many, she was exonerated of all charges and walked out of court, much to the chagrin of law enforcement and government officials, a more popular public figure than ever before.

Shortly after her release, she went to Havana, Cuba in defiance of the travel ban on supposedly free Americans, and was hailed as a great hero before mass crowds that flocked to see the woman who had the audacity to stand-up for justice in America. She eventually returned to the USA and ran for Vice-President on the Communist ticket in 1980 and 1984. She continues to actively fight for justice in a country that incarcerates more people than any other nation in the world. Her prophetic words, "imprisonment has become the response of first resort too many of our social problems," unfortunately rings true in a nation that is obsessed with Old Testament punishment, rather than New Testament forgiveness.

America's suppression of free speech makes a mockery out of its claim to be the freest nation in the world. In 1919, Eugene Debs was sent to prison for distributing anti-war leaflets during World War I. Of course, Mr. Debs was a socialist, which made the government even more determined to put him away for daring to question, not only America's participation in a war that made cannon fodder out of the poor youths who were denied equal opportunity, but who also advocated a system of just economic distribution of wealth.

As a child barely out of diapers, I can only vaguely remember seeing the McCarthy Hearings in storefronts that were displaying that new fangled invention, television. In 1951, McCarthy brought a new dimension to the destruction of people's reputation by attacking them on television before an audience that was often too gullible to question authority. However, thanks to the courage of Edward R. Murrow, this arrogant, bombastic, right-wing buffoon was himself destroyed, just as he had destroyed others. Today, there are no Edward R. Murrow's; rather there are just packs of pretty-faced men and women "news readers" who have no idea of what real journalism is. Today's newscasters spend more time discussing the latest antics of the Kardashians, or reviewing the birth of a child to Tom Cruise and his latest wife, than examining what is going on in the real world in which most of us live. Movie stars and sports figures are the new royalty that we are all supposed to fawn over and worship as the heroes of the modern age.

Over the years, the First Amendment has been slowly chipped away, so America can protect itself from its so-called enemies that want to destroy the wonderful, capitalistic, corporate-loving, religiously controlled-life that permeates through the fabric of the society. As early as 1798, those in power immediately started an assault on the First Amendment when the French and Indian War led to many people questioning the participation of the new nation in what many considered nothing more than a power grab on the part of the new government of the USA. Congress subverted the First Amendment in order to shut-up war critics by passing the Alien and Sedition Act which made it a crime for anyone to publish any false, scandalous and malicious writing against the government. This act led to the prosecution of many newspaper editors who dared question the wisdom of the government.

A variety of laws dealing with sedition, anarchy and conspiracy were passed in the 1800's to suppress abolitionists, suffragists, anti-religious organizations, labour unions and pacifists. In some southern states, these laws even went so far as to ban any attack on people's right to own slaves.

The 1900's were even worse in many ways. For example, well-known activist Margaret Sanger was arrested for giving a speech in which she encouraged people to practice birth control. Labour unions were singled out for special abuse with laws making union meetings illegal. Others laws made strikes and other labour protests illegal.

Protestors were even imprisoned for opposing entry into World War I. One man in particular, the aforementioned Eugene Debs, who just happened to be an avowed socialist, was singled out, because he was a high-profile leader who encouraged workers to unionize and attack the corporate culture of employee slavery. He was sentenced to ten years in prison, disenfranchised, and in spite of the fact that he was born in America, had his citizenship revoked for violating the Espionage Act by telling a large crowd of workers that the capitalists were using them to fuel the American war machine.

When I was in the U.S. Army, we were constantly reminded of how we were defending freedom. I found it particularly hypocritical to be told to defend freedom, and then watch as people were arrested for burning their draft cards. Why should burning a piece of paper lead to a jail sentence in a society that is supposed to guarantee freedom of speech? Then, there was the case in 1969 of Sidney Street that was watched with particular interest by those of us in the army who had the audacity to think for ourselves. When civil rights activist James Meredith was assassinated in Mississippi, a New Yorker named Sidney Street, took his American flag out of a drawer, went onto the street and as he was burning it said, "we don't need no damn flag if they let that happen to Meredith." Street was arrested and charged with violating the New York State Flag Desecration Law, which did not include a prohibition against burning it, but against making disparaging remarks about it. While Americans railed against this obscene affront to the American flag, Street refused to bow before the authorities and the public who dared question his freedom of speech. Appealing all the way to the Supreme Court, his conviction was eventually reversed on a narrow 5-4 vote, as the majority found that the New York law was unconstitutional, because it permitted him to be punished merely for speaking defiant or contemptuous remarks about the American flag. Today's Supreme Court would, no doubt, uphold the conviction as the right wing swing of America has been accomplished thanks to the Supreme Court appointments of Reagan, Bush I and Bush II. Despite the fact that conservative Chief Justice Roberts sided with the people in upholding Obama's health care act, almost all decisions from the Supreme Court follow a strict 5-4 conservative majority division on ideological lines.

Sidney Street is just one of countless average Americans who have valiantly fought for the rights of all by refusing to bow before the mask of tyranny that hides the insidious intent of those who want to lead the USA into the darkness of fascist manipulation and control.

Americans have no real depth of understanding when it comes to any type of freedom, whether it be freedom of press, freedom of assembly, freedom of speech, freedom from illegal search and seizures or freedom of religion. Freedom implies that ideas and beliefs that might be abhorrent to the majority must be jealously protected in order for real freedom to flourish and prosper.

Freedom of speech is the foundation of all freedoms. The right to express ones self affirms the dignity of a person and assures them of reaching their full potential. Without freedom of speech there can be no real advancement of knowledge. I detest the right-wing Christian exclusionary agenda that tries to shove religion and dogmatic patriotism down everyone's throat; however, despite those feelings, I regularly read right-wing commentaries and political trysts, not because I agree with them, but because I want to make sure that I am well informed and able to weigh and consider issues from both sides. Even though I cringe with intellectual agony, I even watch Fox News on occasion on my computer. (I do not own a television, as I found that 450 cable channels only means that the individual has 450 choices of which junk to watch; consequently, all my news comes from newspapers, the internet and magazines.)

Freedom of speech is the wall that keeps the status-quo in check. It allows the average citizen to stand up against the despots of tyrannical manipulation. Unfortunately, most avenues of communication are now controlled by the mass media corporate empires, courtesy of Ronald Reagan's dismantling of the FCC, that are more interested in keeping their advertisers happy than serving the needs of the public which generally run counter to the corporate agenda. Today's ten million dollar a year newscasters are, themselves, part of the elite ruling class that have no concept of how the average working person struggles to survive in a world of corporate thievery and governmental subterfuge.

The much maligned American Civil Liberties Union is much more eloquent than I am when it comes to steadfastly defending the First Amendment. It states that, "mass ignorance is a breeding ground for oppression and tyranny." Unfortunately, today's corporate controlled mass media is often in partnership with the oppressors to institutionalize ignorance for the masses.

CHAPTER 3
THE MOST POTENT DRUG OF ALL

If you support right wing, Christian, patriotic, corporate capitalism in America, your freedom of thought is rarely challenged. However, if you dare to question authority and the corporate capitalistic system of slavery, the defenders of the status-quo will make every attempt possible to bring you to heel. The Black Panthers, the Weatherman, the Students for a Democratic Society, the Socialist Workers Party, the Student Non-Violent Coordinating Committee, the American Indian Movement and even the Southern Christian Leadership Conference have all been on the FBI's targeted hit list at one time or another. For years, J. Edgar Hoover pursued a personal vendetta against Martin Luther King and the SCLC, as well as numerous others who had the gall to question a system based on the economic servitude of the poor to benefit the rich. Ironically, he was also appalled by gay rights activists; no doubt, while he wiggled his toes in his high heels behind his desk, talking to his assumed long-time FBI male lover. Talk about hypocrisy? The man who was supposed to defend people's rights was constantly figuring out ways to abridge them.

This determination to force conformity on the populace did not end with the death of Hoover. In fact, it grew and prospered through the administrations of Ford, Reagan, Bush I, and Bush II, with only a slight aberration during the Carter and Clinton years. Obama, never one to rock the boat, despite what his critics contend, has helped solidify the government's penchant for repression time and time again. Since

9/11, the American public has become more gullible than ever when it comes to supporting a system of economic servitude for the working classes. Now, as a result of the economic meltdown perpetrated by George Bush's incompetence, the gap between the rich and poor has widened even more. Those with jobs acquiesce to corporate pressure to hold-down wages for fear that the executives, who never take a cut in pay, might move their jobs overseas. In fact, among the First World countries, the USA workers make the least and have the fewest benefits. Tell an American that the European worker gets 8 weeks vacation a year, one year of paid maternity leave, guaranteed cost-of-living increases, free health care and a decent pension, and the response from those who would most benefit from a similar system is a parroted. "that's socialism." So, the U.S. politicians and their corporate masters have Americans convinced that socialism is evil. Yeah, sure it is evil – for the rich and powerful, but for the working person, it levels the playing field. What a novel idea – treating the working person like a genuine human being with rights.

In America, persecution of those who do not conform to the norm has been practiced throughout history. This oppression did not even start with the slaves. It actually began with those who came to America in search of religious freedom. These people seeking religious freedom put non-conforming individuals in stocks and burned them at the stake for daring to question the authority of the Bible as interpreted by those in power. In other words, they substituted their own religious oppression for the oppression they had suffered in Europe.

FIGHTING FOR JUSTICE

These same people sanctioned slavery for African Americans, because the Bible indicated that slavery was permitted by almighty God, himself. After all, the Blacks were inferior, because God had angrily made them the tribe of Ham and banished them to Africa, isolating them from the true believers. Therefore, slavery was just a continuation of God's will being done. In later centuries, the descendants of these religious paragons of virtue would help form the Ku Klux Klan.

Even the Civil War did not free the slaves. African-Americans were still relegated to serving the needs of the rich white masters who maintained control of their ability to earn a livelihood. Consequently, under the system of segregation institutionalized in the South, they no longer wore visible chains, but they had invisible chains that locked them into a permanent economic underclass that still had to cater to the whims of the white masters.

Today, liberal thinkers are the prime targets of a variety of right wing groups and individuals who have no tolerance for those who question the status-quo. One right-wing hit man, David Horowitz, even went so far as to publish a book that listed the top 100 academics whom he considered traitors and nothing more than academic terrorists who were polluting the minds of young people against the great American system of government. He followed that with another book entitled, *Indoctrination U* in which he laments about the indoctrination of students in leftist ideas. Of course, he conveniently does not mention the indoctrination practiced by the right wing in the schools, corporations, political organizations and church pulpits of America.

Horowitz is only one of a variety of people and organizations dedicated to destroying independent thought by America's youth. After all, if the poor, who serve as cannon fodder to fight the wars for the rich, were to question why they should fight for a system that permanently relegates them to subservient status, the Bush twins, the Cheney girls and the children of legislators might have wound up serving the cause of freedom in Afghanistan or Iraq. Can you imagine how many wars there would be if the children and grandchildren of people serving in Congress or the Administration were guaranteed a spot on the front lines of all wars?

Horowitz has even helped set-up right-wing watch groups on many campuses, which encourage students to take notes or record suspicious professors. In other words, the conservative students are out to see that professors feel intimidated not to ridicule any American war, use Marxist theology or assign readings that might be considered anti-American.

This intimidation has led many university administrators, particularly in Texas, to develop what they consider a specific guideline as to how professors are supposed to make sure they do not overtly express their views in a way that might indoctrinate the students toward radical ideas.

In some Pennsylvania universities, they have even gone so far as to indicate that irrelevant political material be excluded from lectures and discussions. The list of professors on the right-wing hit lists grows each day as many are being denied tenure, losing jobs or promotions and access to research grants.

The irony is that the people who are encouraging a balanced curriculum only consider it balanced if it is tilted toward right-wing thought and ideology. There is no mention by these supporters of capitalism that in order for fairness and the intellectual thought process to be fully developed, economic departments should have an equal number of Marxists and socialists to balance the curriculum. How many Geology Departments have an anti-oil professor? How many Political Science Departments have faculty who are anarchists? How many English Departments have teachers who specialize in communist literature? How many religious departments have Buddhists and atheists on the staff?

Across the USA, Republican controlled legislatures are introducing Academic Bills of Rights that purport to guarantee balance in college curricula. In reality, these laws are nothing but covert attempts by right-wingers to give authorities the ability to harass and police faculty to make sure they do not use the classroom to express opinions contrary to the accepted norm as defined by the rich, religious and powerful.

Even the federal government got into the act in 2006 when Secretary of Education, Margaret Spellings, a Bush favourite, appointed a commission to oversee universities and monitor their propensities to support radical thought. People like her fail to realize that the founders of America were all rebels with extremely radical thoughts. What America really needs is the promotion of radicalism in order to solve the monumental problems of an economic system based on greed, not a commission to force colleges and universities into conformity. Americans always talk about how free they are, but they are reviled by anyone who dares stand up to authority.

Since September 11, 2001, the United States government has been leading witch-hunts in the USA and abroad for what it identifies as radicals who are undermining America. Questioning President Bush's policies was tantamount to treason. Then, these same people who never wavered in their support of Bush's so-called war on terror were livid with discontent over fear that Obama would loosen the iron grip of repression. They need not have worried, as he has often gone even further than Bush in repressive tactics. His inhumane use of drone air-strikes all over the world violates any norm of the rules of war.

Wiretaps, illegal detentions of citizens and non-citizens, domestic spying and a host of civil rights violations were carried out in the name of national security by Bush, and now Obama, with the complete support of the majority of the public. When asked if they are willing to give up some of their liberty to fight terrorism, the clueless American public overwhelming responds, "yes." How simple-minded to give up the very thing you are supposed to be fighting to defend.

The persecution of Muslims since September 11, 2001 has been particularly brutal. For example, right after the World Trade Centre attack, the Bush administration ordered the shut down of the Holy Land Relief Foundation in Texas and charged several of its officials with aiding terrorism. What was their evidence? The group gave money to organizations that assisted Hamas, which became the legally elected government of the Palestinians. Of course, the Americans consider Hamas a terrorist organization, because it had the audacity to demand fair treatment of the Palestinians by the Israelis. Again, America encourages democracy, but when the Palestinian people elected a group the Americans did not like, suddenly, democracy is only adequate when a government compliant to the American will is elected. Of course, this same anomaly is also apparent in the USA, as the Republicans refused to work with Obama, because he was a "socialist." Any man who has the audacity to introduce some economic fairness into the equation is called a socialist by the Republicans. This goes all the way back to the New Deal, when Republicans called Roosevelt a communist for introducing Social Security. Then, after the veterans returned from defending democracy in World War II, these same people referred to the GI Bill as welfare.

Fabrication and ignoring the truth seem to be at the heart of the American way of governing, because it is assumed that the typical American is just too dumb to think for himself or herself. Based upon the low voter turnout for most elections, this appears to be a relatively valid assumption.

This fabrication technique can be aptly applied to the totally unnecessary war in Iraq. The mysterious weapons of mass destruction were knowingly fabricated, but they did not stop their lies there. They even went so far as to say that Iraq had something to do with 9/11, which was another giant fabrication that, even today, a large percentage of Americans still believe.

The aforementioned Holy Land Relief Foundation situation was another case of fabrication. For example, the government maintained that the organization had made anti-Semitic statements. Yet, they could produce no tapes from wiretaps or written transcripts that supported that claim. While these people were Muslims, one might logically ask where was the outrage over anti-Semitic statements made by the fundamentalist Christians of America who still blame the Jews for the death of Jesus? The government has never moved to shut down any of these fundamentalist churches that spew out hate like water over Niagara Falls. Verbal attacks on homosexuals, liberals, socialists, communists and a variety of other groups is tolerated, but because the USA is at war with radical Islamists, the public is not supposed to make disparaging remarks about Washington's allies in the so-called war on terror.

One of the leaders of Holy Land Relief and Development, Abu Baker, was purported to have railed against the state of Israel in many of the organizations meetings and writings. Yet, the government could not produce one tape or any written material verifying this charge either. It appears that the government assumes that if they say something is true, then it is true, and there need be no evidence presented. Even if it were true, what is illegal about verbally attacking any country in the world for its shortcomings, just as I am doing in this book?

The United States government shut down the organization and seized all its assets. Several of the members were deported and others harassed as the government vendetta continued unabated. This intimation was intended to send a warning to other organizations that dared stand against policies not endorsed by the U. S. government.

All this done to destroy an organization with the stated aim of finding and implementing practical solutions for human suffering though humanitarian programs that impact the lives of the disadvantaged, disinherited and displaced people suffering from man-made and natural disasters. They provided support to victims in Lebanon, Palestine, Bosnia, Kosovo, Turkey and the United States. I suppose if it had been an organization dedicated to helping corporate America enslave the working people of the world, the government would have left them along, as that is not terrorism. However, an organization that combats the evils of militarism and greed is certainly a threat to the security of the USA, the security of corporate USA, that is.

This anti-Muslim crusade also led to the Bush Administration going after a University of South Florida outspoken supporter of the Palestinian cause right after the 9/11 attacks. Sami Al-Arian suffered a "double Bush" attack since he was a professor at the University of South Florida while George W. Bush's brother, Jeb, was governor of Florida; therefore, he had the feds conducting surveillance on him while the governor of the state was demanding he be fired from his tenured teaching position.

In 1948, as a child, Al-Arian and his family were forcibly removed from their homeland after the creation of Israel. He came to America with his family, and after getting a doctorate, he became a highly respected teacher and researcher.

What was his terrorist activity? He published articles and held conferences to get people to sympathize with the plight of the Palestinian people. In addition, he had four books that the government deemed subversive material. Apparently, Americans must be careful what they read, as the FBI has the right to go to libraries and review records to see what books its citizens are checking out.

Acquitted of most charges, after years in detention, government harassment, and possibly torture, Al-Arian finally agreed to plead guilty to one count of conspiracy for the U.S. Attorney agreeing to dismiss all other charges and requesting leniency. Desperate to put an end to three years of government harassment, imprisonment, solitary confinement and family misery, Al-Arian assumed that his long, tortuous ordeal was finally going to end. Unfortunately, he underestimated the cruelty of the U.S. government.

Immediately after agreeing to deport Al-Arian and end the whole affair, the US Attorney decided to hold Al-Arian as a material witness in other spurious cases that the government intended to bring against so-called terrorists. Dr. Al-Arians own words sum up his predicament much better than I can. "Much of the government's evidence against me consisted of speeches I made, magazines I edited, books I owned, conferences I convened, rallies I attended, interviews I conducted, news I heard and websites I visited. In one case, the evidence consisted of a conversation one of my co-defendants had with me in his dream. It was reminiscent of the thought crimes in Orwell's book *1984*. The scary part was not that these were offered in evidence, but that a federal judge actually admitted them. That is why I am so proud of the jury, who acted as the free people they were and saw through the Big Brother tactics of the government."

So, Al-Arian is just another of the thousands who languish in jails, while the U.S. government continues its pursuit of those who dare to stand up for justice in the land of hypocrisy.

The American government does not serve the needs of the people. It serves the needs of a moneyed oligarchy by constantly keeping the average person preoccupied with mundane issues that serve as distractions from the real problems that face a society that has no compassion for the less fortune who are the grease that oils the machinery of capitalism.

From its inception, the American government has fought to maintain the status-quo and assure that the forces of change are subverted and kept under control. An illustration of this is a witch-hunt that has been going on for years. The so-called War-on-Drugs is an excellent example that gives the government view a monopoly on the dispensation of information.

I am a product of the 60's, when America was undergoing a cultural awakening led by youths who were questioning the norms of a hypocritical society that taught values, but did not practice them. Unlike most of my contemporaries, I have never smoked marijuana, but as a professor at Hunter College of CUNY in the 70's, I did often get high from the residual effects of students who openly smoked pot in the classroom at a time when classroom cigarette smoking was permitted. I saw no difference in students smoking pot and smoking cigarettes.

Of course, there was a big difference economically: one product was a corporate distributed form of cancer, while the other product did not add to the bottom line of a corporation. I found it particularly hypocritical that the power structure constantly attacked the permissiveness of the time that led to the acceptance of drugs as part of the youth culture. Many of these government hypocrites delivered their tirades against the evil of drugs while they held a cigarette in their hands. After a public display of disdain for youthful indiscretions, I am sure many of these same bastions of morality headed down to the bar for a few drinks of the drug of their choice, alcohol. This hypocrisy is at the very heart of a society that has those in power dictating the definition of morality for the rest of us, while they do as they please.

Hypocrisy is as American as apple pie. For example, during the Prohibition era, America's religious leaders helped usher in Prohibition, but that did not preclude them from using wine in communion. I wonder how many ministers slipped a drink of communion wine at various times while the congregation was told to avoid alcoholic spirits. Then there is the case of marijuana. The government has tackled the drug problem through a strategy of demonizing, not just the drugs, but also the people using them. It is not the purpose of this chapter to promote the use of drugs. Unlike many people my age, as mentioned previously, I have never smoked or ingested illegal drugs. In fact, I have never even taken an alcoholic drink, not because I consider myself morally superior, but because of a family history of alcoholism that has instilled fear in me of developing an addiction for alcohol or drugs. However, I find it interesting how the giant pharmaceutical corporations, through advertising on television, promote dependency on drugs by convincing people that there is a pill to solve almost every problem most of us must face. It is perfectly all right to be hooked on legitimate corporate drugs to combat chronic pain, but do not pick up a marijuana joint to ease the pain of glaucoma, because that can be habit-forming. It is permissible to buy a bottle of wine at the local corporate owned liquor store, so you can relax after a hard day slaving for your corporate masters, but do not light up some pot to let the tribulations of the day subside. It is permissible to go to the local drug store and buy a variety of corporate-made, over-the-counter pain-killing drugs, but do not use some weed to ease your pain, because that is not funnelling money into the corporations that must be the beneficiaries of all dollars spent by the consumers of America.

FIGHTING FOR JUSTICE

Marijuana cultivation goes back to the 1600's in America. In fact, it was one of the biggest cash crops for a long time as it was used for a variety of things, especially the making of rope. Mr. "All Men are Created Equal" himself, Thomas Jefferson, grew hemp at his beloved Monticello Plantation where he kept the men slaves busy cultivating crops while he was busy building his wealth by impregnating slave women, then selling the off-springs as slaves to buy some expensive bauble that he coveted.

It was not until the 1920's that smoking marijuana came into vogue after it was discovered by some farmers, who, when they were burning their excess crop would get a euphoric feeling from inhaling the fumes. As word of its euphoric effects spread, more people started using it. The corporate drug makers saw this easy to grow pain-easing product as a possible infringement on their lucrative markets, and immediately set out lobbying the government to do something about this abomination. The religious paragons of virtue had already achieved their goal of legislating morality with the Prohibition Act, now it was time for the pharmaceutical giants to get in on the bandwagon and protect their bottom lines.

The government's front man to lead this fight against the "demon weed" was Harry Anslinger. This was a man who really knew how to get to the top the easy way. He married the daughter of Andrew W. Mellon, the Secretary of the U.S. Treasury. Mellon promptly appointed Anslinger as Commissioner of the Federal Bureau of Narcotics. He was assigned the task of making the public see that smoking marijuana was the worst crime in the country. How did this bigoted, right wing, Christian moralist go about doing this job? Perhaps this quote can summarize his approach. "Most marijuana smokers are Negroes, Hispanics, jazz musicians and entertainers. Their satanic music is driven by marijuana, and marijuana smoking by white women makes them want to seek sexual relations with Negroes, entertainers and others. It is a drug that causes insanity, criminality and death. It is the most violence causing drug in the history of mankind."

This is the same kind of hysterical approach used by the U.S. government today in its inane attempt to fight terrorism and instil fear in the American public. Anslinger was around until 1962, spewing this venom, until John Kennedy finally fired him for insubordination. However, this did not end the frenetic approach to the problem. A hodgepodge of laws makes possession of marijuana a felony in one state, while it might be nothing more than a misdemeanour in some states, carrying no jail time at all.

Although the laws have moderated over the years, the emphasis on criminalizing possession of marijuana continues in the USA, while the majority of the world takes a more sane approach. At one time, the law actually recommended the death penalty for anyone selling marijuana to a minor. Therefore, an eighteen year old, selling a joint to a seventeen year old could have been strapped in "Old Sparky" and dispatched to that great marijuana patch in the sky.

It might be interesting to note that in the 1970's Anslinger was suffering from a number of debilitating and painful ailments, and; although there is no proof he ever used marijuana, it was verified that he used another addictive drug, morphine, to ease his agony. Naturally, he is in heaven, and will no longer have to worry about marijuana smokers as they will all go to hell.

The asinine war on drugs, like the war on terrorism, will never succeed as long as the root causes of problems are not addressed by a government that is indifferent to the suffering of its own people and tries to enslave the world to a system of inequity that maintains a power base for the rich and powerful.

Insanity does not afflict the marijuana user, but it is prevalent among the state and federal governments that enforce harsh laws on users who should get addiction treatment rather than jail sentences. Let me use just one example of how short sighted and vindictive this whole approach is. Many years ago, when doing research for an article I was writing, I came across an extremely interesting case of law-enforcement misplaced priorities. In 1989, the Morgan County Alabama Drug Task Force hired a convicted felon to entrap people by offering to sell them pot at a bargain price. One purchaser was Vietnam veteran, Douglas Gray, who after buying a small amount of marijuana, was arrested, convicted and sentenced to life, then shipped off to a maximum-security prison that housed Alabama's worst offenders. Gray's wife, distraught over the affair, attempted suicide. I wonder how many Alabama corporations were polluting the air and streams of the state, while these defenders of justice were busy catching a pot smoker?

FIGHTING FOR JUSTICE

Gray's punishment is not unusual at all. In fact, it is estimated that 50% of all American prison inmates are incarcerated for drug or drug-related crimes. In some states, the penalty for having one marijuana plant is life in prison. Meanwhile, it is legal for someone like Virginia Tech mass murderer, Seung Hui Cho, to walk into a gun shop and buy lethal automatic weapons. In America, there are more deaths from guns than marijuana, but do not even think about denying people the right to go down to their local gun shop to buy an AK-47, as that would be an abridgment of their coveted 2nd Amendment rights to always be "packing."

Drugs can be detrimental to an individual's health and sanity. However, a nation that is so obsessed with punishing the drug user with obscene prison sentences rather than offering rehabilitative services is itself on the road to insanity. The war on drugs was lost the day it was declared. There is something psychotic about a nation that will hand life sentences to possessors of one ounce of marijuana, while turning a blind eye to those who rob people every day in the banks and on Wall Street.

In a culture that makes purchasing automatic weapons as easy as ordering a hamburger at McDonald's, while having a joint in your pocket can get you life in prison, one might logically assume that those making the moral decisions in America are high on the most potent drug of all, "power."

CHAPTER 4
INCARCERATION NATION

In America, the concept of class distinction extends to the justice system. Those who have power and wealth receive fines and light sentences, while the middle class, and especially the poor, are thrown in the slammer. California even has a program that allows some prisoners to buy their way into better jail accommodations. For the select few of the wealthy who are actually convicted of a non-violent crime, California will arrange for a special jail cell that is described as safe and clean for $82 per day. Obviously, only the wealthy and powerful are afforded this type of pay a fee for justice that probably includes a concierge and room service.

The American Constitution guarantees equal justice under the law, but from the very beginning of the country, bail privileges were always available for the wealthy, while the poor had to wait for trial locked in a cell. Until the 1960's, those who could not afford legal representation were often even denied the right to an attorney.

In a country that brags about its human rights record, the very idea that a person with money can get better jail accommodations violates the concept of equal justice under the law. Every prisoner, regardless of race or economic class, deserves to be incarcerated in a humane, sane and safe environment.

Ironically, even the masses seem to believe that famous people deserve special treatment, as years of conditioning have made the majority of Americans look at entertainers and government leaders as royalty who must be put on a pedestal and venerated. Why, in a country that proclaims the supremacy of equality, does the President have to be referred to as Mr. President? Why do Senators or Congressmen have the term Honourable in front of their names? Why is a judge referred to as "His or Her Honour?" Why are Cabinet members referred to as "Mr. or Madam Secretary?"

Paris Hilton is an excellent example of how the rich, powerful and famous are afforded special dispensation when it comes to serving time. When she was sentenced to 45 days, the sentence was almost immediately cut in half when the judge realized that he was not showing this scion of privilege the respect she deserved due to her pedigree. Consequently, he cut the sentence in half. While all this was occurring, the courts and government officials were inundated with admonitions from her many fans who insisted she was receiving an unjustly harsh sentence. These same celebrity worshipping morons would have sit in sombre silence had Paris been a poor, black teenager from the south-central Los Angeles ghetto who had been arrested for drunk driving. Consequently, it is not only the wealthy who think they are due special privileges, but also the ignorant, celebrity worshipping middle class and poor people who believe there is something special about the wealthy and powerful. Her release by the Los Angeles County Sheriff, after serving only three days, created a furor. To the credit of the judge, he ordered her back to jail. She dissolved into tears and hysterics over what she termed the judge's unfairness. Apparently, she forgot that she had already had her sentenced cut in half.

What was even more appalling than her light sentence was the media frenzy. I was particularly revolted when I turned on an American news channel, and the lead story was about Paris Hilton being ordered to serve an appalling 45 days in jail. Meanwhile, the second story of the evening was about four soldiers being killed in Iraq. The American soldiers in Iraq, who were watching that newscast should have realized what their sacrifice actually meant to the people back home. As Nicholas Van Hoffman once said during the Vietnam War, the soldiers should turn to the politicians, hand them their guns and say, "if the war is so damn important, here is my gun, give it to one of your children or grandchildren and let them fight it."

American justice is based on socio-economic status. Paris Hilton's time was served in a country-club cell reserved for "high profile" inmates. As mentioned previously, California is one of many states that now allow the wealthy and almost exclusively white inmates, not convicted of a felony, to arrange to pay for better and safer accommodations. Meanwhile, the poor and disenfranchised get longer sentences, more sparse accommodations, filthy conditions and violent environments.

When Zsa Zsa Gabor slapped a cop in 1994, she was sentenced to a whopping three days in jail, but was allowed to serve that time treated like royalty for the princely sum of $85 per day. Would the same judge have given an African-American woman from Watts a three-day sentence and the option of serving her time in a country club jail?

America has more people incarcerated than any other country on earth. How laughable to be told that Americans are the freest people in the world by the moronic politicians of right wing ideology. In 2005, statistics indicated that over seven million people (nearly one in every forty-two people in the USA at the time) were in prison, either on probation or on parole. With only 5% of the world's population, the USA has 25% of the world's prison population. Since 1970, the incarceration rate in America has increased over 600%. These figures do not include the large number of so-called "terrorist detainees" housed by US authorities in various gulags in America and other foreign locations.

Ethnically, the USA prison population is 64% Latino and African American, while those two ethnic groups make up only 25% of the total population. Economically, nearly 90% of the prison population can be defined as those who were born into poverty. Another survey found that 68% of African-Americans and 60% of Hispanics under the age of eighteen knew someone who had been shot. In my opinion, based upon my own experiences in south-central Los Angeles, the statistics are probably understated. In one particular school where I spent a great deal of time, there were no less than three shootings in one year, and one of them occurred while kids were on the playground, as an assailant simply rode by the playground, sighted a target getting ready to bat in a baseball game and opened-up with an automatic weapon. On Monday mornings, many of my students would recount harrowing weekend tales of shootings and gang violence. While the United States spends billions to incarcerate people, build weapons of mass destruction and give rich people obscene tax breaks, the plight of the disadvantaged is ignored with the admonition, "anyone can make it in America, if they just make an effort." I am sure that was probably said by some politician born into a family of wealth and privilege.

The aforementioned "war on drugs" and the "mandatory sentencing laws" have been the single most dominant factors in the exploding U.S. prison population. In 1984, there were only 50,000 drug offenders incarcerated. Today, the number is over 500,000. Is anyone really naïve enough to believe all these people are hardened "drug kingpins" dealing death on every street corner? Many of them are just hard core users, who support their own habit by selling drugs. Many of them are pulling life sentences, just because they are three time losers, who in some states, like California, get an automatic life sentence for a third felony conviction.

One in every eleven people in prison is serving a life sentence. Many of these people are not there for murder. They are there for minor felony offences that were third strikes. Take the case of Santos Reyes, who is in California's Folsom Prison serving from 25 years to life, because his third conviction was for taking a driver's licence test under an assumed name. Since the crime is a felony and was his third strike, the judge was left no leeway in the sentencing.

FIGHTING FOR JUSTICE

Gladys Wilson, a poor Detroit woman, was convicted of being an accessory to robbery in 1978. She pled guilty when she was promised a sentence of life with the proviso that she would be eligible for parole in ten years. During that ten-year period, the political climate changed with the election of "get tough on criminals" President Ronald Reagan. By 1988, the state of Michigan decided that life in prison meant life in prison. So, Gladys sat in the slammer until 2005, when she was released after serving 27 years of a sentence she was assured would only be 10 years.

America also incarcerates more young people than any other place in the world. In 2006, there were nearly 2400 people serving life in prison who had been under 18 at the time of the alleged crimes. It is not unusual for children as young as 13 to be given life sentences in a country that proclaims itself the most humane nation on earth. They fail to mention that this humaneness is almost exclusively reserved for the rich and powerful.

Ronald Reagan's mantra of "privatize it and let the wonders of the free market work its magic" was even extended to prisons in the 1980's. Today, one of America's biggest growth industries is private prisons operated by corporations that promise to house "the malcontents of society" for less money than the state. Are these corporate run gulags interested in rehabilitating prisoners, or are they interested in minimizing the costs of housing them in order to increase the return to their stockholders? The very idea of running a prison to make a profit is itself cruel and unusual punishment. However, in America, the word "profit" is a holy and revered word of equal status with the word, "Jesus."

Human Rights Watch estimates that around 250,000 U.S. prisoners suffer from mental disorders. Yet, mental health programs are being cut. Thanks to the inhumane release of mental patients on the streets of American by Ronald Reagan, prisons are now the new mental institutions.

A recent California report indicated that nearly half of all prisoners are illiterate, but there is very little vocational or academic training available for inmates. When released from prison, the punishment for these people does not end, as they can be denied welfare payments, food stamps and veterans benefits. I find the last one particularly distasteful, as in the few instances where Congressmen and government officials have actually served some jail time for felonies, when released, they do not lose their lavish government pensions. What is next, taking away the meagre social security benefits of old people convicted of jaywalking?

The USA has always had a love affair with the death penalty, and is one of the few countries left with that archaic approach to justice. The Old Testament adage, "an eye for an eye and a tooth for a tooth" is a favourite Bible passage for the Christian right wing and the politicians who cater to this barbaric need to exact harsh punishment on transgressors. These same moral guardians conveniently forget Jesus' admonition "to turn the other cheek."

FIGHTING FOR JUSTICE

America has been demanding its pound of flesh in retribution since its inception, as this so-called Christian nation is more interested in exacting revenge than showing a humane side by extending the hand of compassion and offering the chance for redemption. "Lock um up and throw away the key" has been in vogue for years, particularly since Ronald Reagan decided that poverty and prejudice were no excuse for crime. Those relegated to the lower rungs of society to serve the needs of the powerful, rich and privileged must realize that service to the master class is a small price to pay for the freedom they enjoy in the great land of opportunity called America. People must remember that according to the Constitution, "all men are created equal." It may be a little difficult for the child living in a squalid public housing project in Watts to actually think he or she is born equal to the child in Beverly Hills, but the media and the politicians do everything they can to perpetuate this ridiculous myth.

Everyone knows that George Bush is a man of principle who always did what he thought was right. When he was governor of Texas, he certainly thought every death penalty was deserved and refused to commute any death sentences. Mercy is a word that this man, who claims that his greatest inspiration is Jesus Christ, seems to have no understanding of whatsoever. In fact, he set the modern day record for executions while he was governor of Texas, only to be passed by his successor, Rick Perry.

When asked about the chance of making a mistake in administering the death penalty, George "Law and

Order for the Poor Suckers" Bush arrogantly stated that the state of Texas did not make mistakes when applying the death penalty. How fortunate that another Republican governor did not feel that way. When thirteen Illinois inmates on death row were exonerated of their crimes, Republican Governor Ryan commuted all death row sentences to life in prison when it came out that many inmates had been tortured into confessing by various police departments.

George Bush, with his decision to not treat prisoners of war as prisoners of war, but rather to call them enemy combatants, so that the Geneva Convention could be ignored, institutionalized torture in America. Guantanamo Bay is as big a blight on America as Auschwitz was on Germany.

If a foreign army invaded America, you would hear calls from all quarters to resist and use any means possible to fight back. Yet, when America invaded Afghanistan and Iraq, those who fought back were branded as criminals. One of those people who fought back was a 15-year-old boy named Omar Khadr, who allegedly lopped a hand grenade that "might" have killed a U.S. soldier. He was taken to a nearby camp where, according to several sources, in spite of being wounded, he was interrogated and tortured. In 2002, he was transferred to the gulag at Guantanamo Bay and held in solitary confinement. The USA ignored all international protocols in regards to holding children captured in combat. Even the Nuremberg War Trials for Nazi criminals refused to charge anyone under the age of 18. However, America does not make mistakes, as it is as omnipotent as the God it supposedly serves.

FIGHTING FOR JUSTICE

Finally, after being held as a prisoner (excuse me, detainee) for 8 years, in 2010, he was forced to accept a plea deal by a military tribunal that sentenced him to 10 years in prison.

I suppose God looks down with pride on a country like the USA that calls itself the beacon of liberty. As it fills its prisons with the poor, the disadvantaged, the dissidents and the ethnic minorities, perhaps it should also call itself, "the incarceration nation."

CHAPTER 5
CLARENCE DARROW VERSES THE CHURCH

<u>Two Philosophical Indian Tales</u>

Vice-President Lyndon Baines Johnson received the following message on February 11, 1962 from a Native American chief: *We are stuck on reservations with high unemployment, low wages for those who are employed, sub-standard housing, no health care and a generation that spends more time in jail than hunting buffalo. Be careful with your immigration laws. We were careless with ours, and look at us now.*

Two white government men were on a reservation, talking with a chief who had just turned 101 years of age. They asked him about all the technological advances initiated by the white man, and all the new wealth brought to the country through a system of capitalism that offered everyone the opportunity to achieve great wealth. The old chief smiled, shook his head and said, "the white man found the land with Indians running free. We had no taxes, no debt, an abundant supply of free food, free medical care from the tribe's medicine man and we spent all day fishing and hunting. Then, at night, we were well rested for unlimited love-making. Only the white man is dumb enough to think he could improve on a system like that."

Many people like to think that slavery ended in America after the Civil War. In fact, it was expanded. Today, it is not only African-Americans who are slaves, but all the races that must toil for the corporations that refuse to share the bounty with the real workers who produce the wealth that is funnelled into the hands of the few who sit in the board rooms, drawing obscene salaries, receiving exorbitant perks and demanding more of the workers as they cut back on their health and retirement benefits. Americans are too wrapped up in capitalist dogma to realize that in order to have a leisure class, you must have an exploited working class.

In the Middle Ages, the serfs were ruled by the lords of the manner. Today, the serfs are called employees, and the lord of the manner is the CEO and his administrative henchmen who keep the machinery of exploitation oiled with the sweat of the working people.

Ronald Reagan, voted by a gullible public in 2006 as the greatest American, turned his back on the working people by setting out to destroy the labour unions. In 1981, he fired the air traffic controllers, who had unionized; thereby, making it clear to corporate America that the U.S. government had given the green light to exploitation of the working masses. No longer did employers have to worry about organized labour, because the government itself had decided to destroy the power of the unions.

Rather than voting Reagan the greatest American, the public should have selected one of the hundreds of individuals who helped organize exploited workers into unions to fight people like Reagan who saw any attempt by the working people to organize and demand fair treatment as a communist plot. Reagan's obsession with communism, led to him nearly bankrupting the country with huge budget deficits fuelled by his lavish defence spending. Ironically, he campaigned on a platform of balancing the budget, but like all Republicans, he demanded huge tax cuts for the rich as soon as he got into office, which led to big deficits.

May Day is celebrated all over the world as a workers holiday, but not in the United States of America, because it is considered a communist holiday. In America, the bosses are glorified and lionized as captains of industry who make America great, while the workers are just useless peons who want to be coddled and pampered.

America's labour leaders have been vilified and demonized for nearly 400 years, as any attempt to improve the working conditions of employees is considered an attack on the capitalist system. This system of servitude has been protected by the government, the courts, the military, the police and when necessary, armed thugs.

A primary example of capitalistic servitude is the use of the Irish in the coal mines right after the Civil War. The Irish were the equivalent of today's exploited Hispanics who serve the elite of America as gardeners, pickers, janitors and manual labourers. The Irish were encouraged to come to America in the 1870's, as the industrialists saw them as cheap labour for the factories and mines that were springing up all over the country. One state in particular, Pennsylvania, was the hub for mining activity. The immigrant Irish flocked to the state.

108   IN THE LAND OF HYPOCRISY

FIGHTING FOR JUSTICE

Wages were not only low, sometimes averaging 80 cents per day, but the working conditions were extremely dangerous with hundreds of deaths every year, and thousands of miners suffering serious injuries. If a miner was killed, the next day, his family would be evicted from their house, so a new worker could be brought in to toil for the company. Those injured and unable to work were also evicted from their homes, as the company was under no obligation to assist a worker who had been hurt on the job. In fact, those injured were even expected to pay their own medical bills.

During one five year period in Schuylkill County alone, nearly 600 men were killed in the mines and almost 2000 seriously injured. One coal company owner offered the following retort, "the company takes risks with its capital. The miners take risks with their lives. That is just the way it is and always will be. If the miners don't like it, they can work somewhere else."

The working conditions and wages for the miners made them virtual slaves to companies that forced them live in rental company houses, buy food from the company store, and usually paid them, not in money, but in company script that could only be used at the aforementioned facilities. In these conditions, it was only natural for the workers to consider organizing in order to exert some power, so they could improve their working and living conditions.

From 1867 until 1878, an organization known as the Molly Maguire's grew out of the desperation felt by the workers abused by the coal companies. The group has often been reviled by historians for being a terrorist organization. (Doesn't that sound familiar?) Of course, corporations using mercenary thugs to intimidate the workers and polluting the environment was not terrorism. It is the same today, with people practicing sabotage against corporations that pollute the environment being called eco-terrorists while the real eco-terrorists are the corporations that continue to spew their filth in the air we breath and the water we drink, aided by governments that are bought and paid for by them.

Crimes attributed to the Molly Maguire's included murder, assault, sabotage, arson and robbery. However, attributing all these crimes perpetrated against the coal companies to the Molly Maguire's rest primarily on the testimonies of a coal company owner and a Pinkerton private detective who worked for the coal companies. Other credible sources were hard to come by.

Through an organizing drive, eventually 85% of the anthracite coal miners joined the union. However, while the miners were busy organizing, so were the coal companies. Through the efforts of Franklin B. Gowen, the Schuylkill County District Attorney, who also happened to be the President of the largest coal company in America, the owners got together and formed a coal employers association. Gowen told the owners it was time to declare war on unions and exterminate them. On the night of December 10, 1876, three Molly Maguire's were attacked in their houses. One man was killed and a woman was dragged outside and executed. Violence on both sides spread rapidly over the next few years as a tit-for-tat mentality took hold.

The owners hired the infamous Pinkerton Detective Agency to assist in destabilizing the union through intimidation and subterfuge. While the railroad and coal mine owners rode in luxuriously appointed private rail cars, the miners were told they would have to take a 20% pay cut in order to make the companies more profitable. (Sounds like today's corporations that generate billions in profits, raise the executives salaries and then either lay off workers or ask them to take pay cuts to keep the companies profitable and competitive in the global economy.)

Finally, the state militia was called-up to patrol the streets of Schuylkill County and intimidate the miners. Ministers decried the social unrest and encouraged the miners to return to work, and the so-called "free press" virulently attacked the union as a precursor to anarchy. Assailed from all sides, the union was finally set-up for a fall when Gowen got himself appointed special prosecutor. Twenty-six union leaders were arrested and charged with conspiracy, when, in effect, the government turned the whole judicial process over to the coal companies and their representatives. Pennsylvania changed their conspiracy law to read as follows, "any confederation to increase or depress the price of any commodity, whether labour, merchandise, or anything else, is indictable as a conspiracy under the laws of Pennsylvania. Depending on the seriousness of the offence, it is the judge's option to assign punishment, which may include the death penalty."

FIGHTING FOR JUSTICE

Gowen inundated his press friends with stories of union misdeeds, but the papers rarely did any independent investigations on their own. Ultimately, the state turned the entire prosecution over to the companies' attorneys while the state simply supplied the courtroom and the places where the so-called conspirators were hanged. Yes, you read it correctly. On the testimony of one Pinkerton detective who had supposedly been an undercover operative in the union, nineteen men were hanged. The union was broken, and the history of the whole affair was written by the victors who claimed the Molly Maguire's were simply a pack of anarchists.

A few years later in 1886 over 200,000 workers went on strike in the Midwest. At a lumberyard on Chicago's South Side, where workers were demonstrating against unfair labour practices, the notoriously thuggish Chicago police fired into the crowd, killing four demonstrators. This culminated in 80,000 people showing up in Chicago's Haymarket Square the next day to demand an eight-hour workday. Eked on by politicians, newspapers and corporations, police officers opened fire on the crowd of workers demanding an eight-hour day, when someone supposedly threw a bomb at the police. There was never any evidence that a bomb was actually thrown; although, there were six police officers killed, but all but one apparently died from gunshot wounds, apparently fired by their fellow officers. The authorities, serving the interests of Chicago's ruling classes, filed no charges against the police but rounded up radicals, seized union records and closed socialist and labour newspapers, then arrested and convicted a group of union leaders, whom they deemed anarchists, for murder. The judge imposed the death sentence on seven of them and gave a life sentence to one. Albert Parsons, August Spies, George Engel and Adolph Fischer were strung up within a few weeks of the sentence to make a lasting impression on any workers who still harboured thoughts of supporting a union. Three others had their sentences commuted to life in prison.

In America, law enforcement and the judiciary have traditionally been an ally of the ruling class that sees unions as a communist abomination that threatens their stranglehold on labour upon whose backs their fortunes are built. One man who understood this was Joe Hill. In 1879, Joe Hill was born in Sweden. He immigrated to the USA in 1902 and became a migrant worker, roaming from New York to California. While working on the San Pedro docks near Los Angeles, he joined the fledgling Dock Worker's Union (Industrial Workers of the World). He rose through the ranks and became one of the union's chief organizers. He came up with the phrase "pie in the sky" which referred to the tendency of religion to tell the oppressed that they would get their reward in the hereafter. In 1914, Hill took a job as a labourer at the King Silver Mine in Park City, Utah. His reputation for organizing workers preceded him. The mine owners of the area were fearful that he would start a Utah union. Having operated a business in Park City in the early 1980's, I found it interesting that no one in the city had ever heard of Joe Hill, or that there was no commemorative plague honouring him. Why would he be remembered you might ask?

FIGHTING FOR JUSTICE

Perhaps the question should be, why should he be remembered in a notoriously anti-union state, and in a country where warmongers like Ronald Reagan, George Bush and Dick Cheney are venerated, while those who try to lift-up the working people are branded socialists or communists?

Joe Hill spent most of his life in pursuit of fairness for the real working people of the United States, but in doing so, he was signing his own death warrant, because powerful corporate interests saw him as a threat to their economic domination. On January 10, 1914, two masked men killed John Morrison and his son Arling in a Salt Lake butcher shop. One of the killers was shot by Arling with a shotgun. Nothing was stolen, and since Morrison was a former police officer, it was at first assumed that it was an act of revenge from some of the many enemies he had made over the years.

What was the connection to Hill? That same night, a jealous husband in an argument shot the notorious lady's man, Joe Hill. Hill went to a Salt Lake hospital and was treated for a bullet wound (not a shotgun wound). After arresting twelve different men for the crime, only to have them come up with solid alibis, it was learned by the authorities, from an anonymous source, that the famous union organizer, Joe Hill was in town that night and had been to the hospital for the treatment of a gunshot wound. Just as it is today, Salt Lake was virulently anti-union; consequently, the mere fact that Hill was a famous organizer made his indictment not only convenient for the police, but also extremely advantageous for the anti-union businessmen who saw an opportunity to rid the country of what they termed just another anarchist.

Hill denied any involvement in the crime, and produced a coat that showed he had been shot in the back; therefore, how could Arling Morrison shoot him after Arling was already dead? He had also been shot with a small calibre weapon, not a shotgun. In addition, the police did not bother to check on the four other men who had been treated for gunshot wounds that night at the hospital. Morrison's own brother, who had been outside the shop during the crime, when he saw Joe Hill at the police station, said, "that ain't the guy," but his testimony changed at the trial, after coaching by the DA. The fact that Hill did not even know Morrison, and that there was no motive whatsoever for the crime, did not sway the jury from deliberating only a short time before returning a guilty verdict. Once again, a champion of the working man was silenced in the land of hypocrisy.

An article in a socialist newspaper read: *Owing to the prominence of Mr. Morrison, there had to be a goat. Hill was an itinerant tramp, a foreigner and worst of all, a union organizer for the IWW; therefore, he had no right to live anyway, and his conviction made it possible to not only close a case of murder, but get rid of a thorn in the side of the powerful mine barons who run the state.* Despite pleas for mercy from all over the world, the state of Utah executed Hill on November 19, 1915.

Hill had joked that he would not be caught dead in Utah. Heeding his wishes, friends arranged to have his body cremated and sent to Chicago, where his ashes were sent to the IWW local in a large envelope. The United States government, because of what it said was virulent, anarchist and subversive potential, seized the envelope containing Joe Hill's ashes. What was subversive about an envelope? A caption affixed to it said: *The ashes of Joe Hill, murdered by the capitalist class, November 19, 1915.* The government finally turned the ashes over to the IWW in 1988, but not the envelope.

THE PREACHER AND THE SLAVE
by
JOE HILL

Long-winded preachers come out every night,
Try to tell you what's wrong and what's right;
But when asked how 'bout something to eat,
They will never answer in voices so sweet.

You will eat bye and bye,
In that glorious land above the sky;
Work and play, live on hay,
You'll get pie in the sky when you die.

And the Salvation Army they play,
And they sing and they clap and they pray,
Till they get all your coin on the drum,
Then, they'll tell you when you're a bum.

Holly rollers and jumpers come out,
And they holler and they jump and they shout,
Give your money to Jesus, they say
He will cure all diseases today.

FIGHTING FOR JUSTICE

If you fight hard for children and wife,
Try to get something good in this life,
You're a sinner and a bad man, they tell,
When you die, you will sure go to hell.

Workingmen of all countries, unite
Side by side for freedom we will fight,
When the world and its wealth we have gained,
To the grafters we will sing this refrain:

You will eat bye and bye,
When you've learned how to cook and how to fry;
Chop some wood, 'twill do you good,
Then you'll eat in the sweet bye and bye.

Let us take another look at how the miners of America have been particularly oppressed by the corporate giants that wield the heavy hand of repression. In 1914, the miners in the Colorado coalfields tried to join the United Mine Workers of America Union. When the minors were refused the opportunity to unionize, they promptly went on strike. They were immediately evicted from their company owned houses in the middle of one of the coldest Aprils in Colorado history. Sitting up a tent city on public property in Ludlow, they were vilified by the politicians, the press and the corporate power brokers. At the urging of the Colorado Fuel and Iron Company, the owners, in collusion with county and city officials, hired the Felts Detective Agency to suppress what they termed socialist anarchy. The main weapon of fear was a specially equipped armoured car dubbed "The Death Dealer," that roamed about the tent city spewing bullets through the tops of tents in order to scare the miners and their families. Refusing to be intimidated, the minors dug foxholes in the floors of the tents, so they could stay below the flying bullets.

One morning, at 10:00 AM, the order was given to remove all squatters from the tent city. Coal company guards, strike breakers and hired thugs ringed the area and started indiscriminately firing into tents. The armoured machine gun also opened fire and the screams of women and children were barely audible over the constant roar of gunfire that suddenly stopped as a group of men poured kerosene onto the tents. Then, the gun fire started again and the tents went up in flames. When the smoke had cleared, twenty-six people were dead. These brave defenders of capitalism, in addition to sixteen men and women, killed 10 children, aged three months to eleven years. Not a single person was ever arrested for the massacre. Oh, by the way, the owners of the Colorado Fuel and Iron Company just happened to be one of America's best-known and most philanthropic families, the Rockefellers.

One of my favourite movies is John Sayle's classic film, *Matewan*. Unlike most American films, it was actually a movie with a great social message; consequently, very few people were interested in seeing it, so it tanked at the box office. After all, it did not have gratuitous sex, car chases, intense violence or anything being blown up, so what possible value could it have to a public that is more interested in who won on American Idol than how many U.S. soldiers were killed in the latest American adventure to bring corporate democracy to some third world country?

FIGHTING FOR JUSTICE

The whole Matewan affair started when one lone, determined miner decided to join the union. This one miner was a threat to the coal company, so they hired the infamous Baldwin-Felts Detective Agency to send some thugs down to the company house where the miner lived. They strong armed his wife and set the furniture out in the middle of the road. Upon hearing of what had been done, hundreds of other miners immediately joined the union. Unlike previous incidents, the police chief, Sid Hatfield and the mayor, Collins Testerman of Matewan, West Virginia sided with the miners. Hatfield urged the coal companies to order the Felt detectives out of town, but his pleas were ignored.

On May 19, 1920, the president of Felts himself, Thomas Felts, along with his brothers Albert and Lee, arrived in Matewan to evict all miners who had joined the union. When word of the thuggish tactics used by these brazen corporate gendarmes reached the miners, they grabbed their guns and asked Hatfield to do something about this act of barbarity. Hatfield, along with several miners and Mayor Testerman, went to the company houses and pleaded with the Felts' detectives to stop their actions until things could be talked over in a more humane and less confrontational manner, since they had not gone through proper channels to get eviction notices issued by a local magistrate.

No one knows who fired the first shot, but as Thomas Felts glared at Hatfield, refusing to bow to local authorities, a shot rang out. Then, all hell broke lose, and after less then a one minute gun battle, Al and Lee Felts, along with seven other detectives, two miners and Mayor Testerman were dead. For once, it appeared that the workers had come out on top.

The battle made Sid Hatfield a revered figure to union men and women all over America, but only fifteen months after the gun battle, Baldwin-Felts detectives retaliated by assassinating Hatfield on the steps of the county courthouse. Once again, the barons of greed who run America would show no mercy for anyone siding with the working people.

However, Hatfield's death led to outrage on the part of the oppressed miners, and one of the most glorious moments in the American labour movement followed. Fed up with the years of brutal exploitation, over 10,000 miners got their guns and started marching to Mingo and Logan Counties to demand that the largest coal companies acquiesce to unionization.

At about the same time, the famous or infamous sheriff of Logan County, depending on your point of view, Don Chafin, who also owned the Chafin Mine, visited the headquarters of the Vice-President of the West Virginia miners' local, Bill Petry, and told him to keep union members out of Logan County, if he knew what was good for him. Chafin further intonated that he would have armed men waiting for the union people if they tried to unionize the county's coal mines.

Petry is said to have smiled broadly and replied, "Hell, Don. Why wait, you got a gun and so do I."

Both men went for their revolvers and Petry shot the sheriff right above the heart. Chafin placed a hand over the hole and without firing a shot, calmly walked to the nearby hospital where he was treated and released. Chafin returned to Logan County and organized a posse that sit up on a ridge near the county line, waiting for the arrival of the armed miners. For ten days, Chafin's men and the miners fought a fierce battle known locally as the Battle of Blair Mountain in which 47 men were killed and hundreds injured. As the battle raged, the President of the United States, Warren G. Harding, demanded that all miners disperse and retire to their homes and abandon their demands for undemocratic unionization. As one might expect, Harding was a Republican who once said, "the business of America is business."

The miners ignored Harding and the President ordered federal troops into the state to, as he stated, "restore law and order and to make sure the union did not take over and create a state of anarchy." He also ordered army planes loaded with gas bombs and machine guns to fly to the state under the command of renowned general, Billy Mitchell.

Out-gunned and out-manned, the miners eventually conceded that they could not fight both the mine owners and the federal government that was backed by tanks, airplanes and army troops determined to protect the capitalist exploiters. 982 people were arrested on various charges including murder, accessory to murder and treason. (That is correct; it was apparently considered treason to stand-up to corporate power.) Some of the trials took place in the same courthouse where the slave rebellion leader, John Brown, was convicted of treason and hanged.

FIGHTING FOR JUSTICE

Lack of any credible evidence led to the acquittal of most people. However, the government was able to railroad a few minor participants like Reverend J.W. Wilburn and his son, John. After years of ministering to the poor who toiled in the mines, the reverend, according to some Felts detectives said to a crowd of miners, "it is time to lay down the Bible and pick up the gun." On the testimony of three company-hired detectives, these two men were sentenced to eleven years in prison.

Backed by the U.S. government and its military might, the miners were again crushed by the powerful and wealthy in yet another battle for human dignity. As for the assassins of Sid Hatfield, no one was ever arrested or prosecuted.

Americans are told that class warfare does not exist in the USA, as everyone has equal opportunity. This has always been a lie. In the past, there were three distinctive classes: the poor, the middle class and the rich. Today, the middle class is rapidly disappearing as more of this group falls into the poor category.

George Bush and his Republican brethren maintained they helped the middle class by cutting taxes, but in the process, they rewarded the rich with even greater tax savings, and created the biggest budget deficits in history, until Barrack Obama came along, and in order to avert another great depression, had to funnel massive amounts of money into a corrupt system that was ready to collapse. Perhaps it would have been better if the system had collapsed. As, like Franklin Roosevelt, all Obama did was save a capitalistic system that continues to enslave the workers of America to the corporate bottom line. If the system had been allowed to collapse, maybe the people would have finally gotten enough courage to stand up to the corporate oligarchs who run the country and demanded a system based on equality of opportunity.

While the rich caused the crisis, the solution, as usual, was to ameliorate the problem by burdening the middle class with the tab for saving capitalism. Meanwhile, the Republican response to the huge deficits is to cut social welfare programs, while spending lavishly on wars of conquest and corporate welfare. Then, they top it off by suggesting, as always, that the solution to every problem is to cut taxes even more for the rich. Through it all, the clueless American public continues to wave the flag and shout "hallelujah" every time someone invokes the righteousness of America as God's ordained dispenser of justice throughout a world.

Because of this obscene drive to reward the rich at the expense of the middle class and poor, all of America has become a Matewan. There are more wage slaves today that ever before, and the corporate forces that rule the political system intend to consolidate and hold their power until every American is subdued and forced to pay penance to the almighty corporation.

Since the election of Ronald Reagan, the federal government has drastically cut social welfare programs, union protections and, in the case of Republicans, even tried to destroy social security, all while awarding the rich with huge tax cuts which has led to the greatest gap between the rich and poor in the entire First World. The American government has waged a war on the middle class and poor, and with the election of George "Bring-um On" Bush, the rich and powerful declared total victory. Then, when Obama could not get any meaningful legislation passed as a result of Republican obstructionism in Congress, the American public put Republicans back in control of Congress, because Obama could not get things completely turned around in 2 years. So, the "wise" American public turned things back over to the very people who caused the whole problem to start with.

As long as the Senate abides by the arcane rule that it takes 60 votes to pass anything, there will never be any real change in the country. Yet, Americans, who have had four Presidents who lost the popular vote and allow a minority of 41 people in a 100 seat Senate to block any legislation, live under the illusion that they are in a democracy. The truth is, the USA was never intended to be a democracy, and it never has been. America was set-up by a bunch of wealthy agri-businessmen who wanted to avoid paying taxes to England. They used the word democracy as a con to get people to go along with a system that was intended to protect the interests of the wealthy.

The greatest safety net the poor have in America is the social security system, but since 1933, the Republicans have fought to dismantle a system they described then and now as pure socialism. However, if you turn the process over to corporate management, they would no longer consider it socialism. There has been no concentrated effort to fix the system for years;

as it is projected that it will go broke by 2040. The simple way to fix the system would be to make social security taxes apply to an entire income, but in order to do that, the rich would have to pay nearly 7% on their entire salary, whereas, social security taxes stop at around $110,100 (as of 2012). Consequently, the rich have always received a huge tax break on social security, and you can be sure that no administration, Democrat or Republican will dare impose the social security tax on a person's entire income. The American social security tax is one of the most regressive taxes in the world, as it takes the most from those who can afford it the least. Again, from the very beginning, the whole social security system was set up to make sure that the middle class had to bear the burden of the tax while allowing those at the top to escape paying their fair share.

The American labour pool is generally over-educated and under-employed. An education no longer guarantees that an individual will get a good paying job. It is estimated that 25% of all workers with college educations are in jobs that do not require a university degree. Even when corporations are banking huge profits, they often layoff workers in an attempt to cut costs more, up productivity and increase their bottom line. Therefore, doing a good job for the corporation can actually be to a worker's detriment. Greed is an infectious disease that spreads like a wildfire. The more a corporation makes, the more it wants to make, and there is never any consideration given to those who toil in the workplace. Rather, the executives, who spend many of their days on the golf course or at the country club enjoying two martini lunches, are lavishly rewarded for the success of the company, while the real workers are expendable and are constantly being asked to produce more for the same or less pay.

After World War II, the unions saw to it that American workers had job security and a reasonable level of pay. By the 1960's almost 40% of Americans were unionized. This guarantee of a fair wage and job security led to the greatest expansion of the middle class in history. The so-called Reagan Revolution ushered in the dismantling of this system of worker protection, and today, for all practical purposes, the entire process has been dismantled. The average American will now have eleven jobs in his or her lifetime, and few of them will have a vested pension plan. Worker pay is being slashed when adjusted for inflation and the burden of health insurance is being shifted from the employer to the employee. Today, health insurance for a family of four can run as high as $1400 a month, and that is still only limited coverage. Meanwhile, the members of Congress, the Executive Branch, the Judiciary and the corporate executives continue to have these benefits provided to them almost free of charge.

The National Labour Relations Board was set-up to make sure that employers did not harass or intimidate employees who wanted to form a union. Through a series of Republican appointments to this board, the tables have been turned, and it is now almost impossible to form a union if the employer really wants to fight it. The employer has a right to appeal any vote to unionize. During this appeal process, the union is not certified. The normal time for an appeal is

2 ½ years; consequently, the employer can engage in all types of nefarious practices while waiting for the case to be heard.

The Smithfield Pork Processing Plant in North Carolina has been able to hold off unionization for years. While appeal after appeal is filed, the workers continue to be harassed, intimidated, injured and even killed as the company puts profits ahead of safety. In 2003, a 25-year-old worker, Glenn Birdsong, was overcome with fumes and killed while climbing down to clean a holding tank. When the North Carolina Division of Occupational Safety and Health fined the company for egregious violations, a stern message was sent to the company. Their fine was a whopping $4300. That was later reduced by 30%, when the company complained about the excessive fine.

The so-called global economy is nothing more than a smoke screen used by American corporations to keep labour in line. The threat of outsourcing has created immense fear for people, as the Third World is used as a pawn to keep American workers in constant fear of losing their jobs; and thereby, fearful of demanding wage and benefit increases. In fact, wage concessions are much more common today than wage increases.

The porous American border with Mexico also serves as a great deterrent to increases in wages and benefits. A constant supply of cheap labour, and the lack of any concentrated effort on the part of the federal government to stem the tide of illegal immigrants affords employers the opportunity to exploit foreign workers and keep American workers in constant fear of losing their jobs should they demand too much from their employers. This tsunami of illegal cheap labour could be stopped immediately if Congress and the President would simply pass a law mandating jail sentences and large fines for those employers who hire undocumented workers. Instead of doing that, they suggest grandiose schemes for building fences that never get built, approve the hiring of more border patrol agents who never get hired or send the National Guard to patrol the borders with no mandate for them to arrest any people who cross into America illegally. In other words, the Congress and the President engage in a game of smoke and mirrors to try and convince the public they are doing something about the problem, when they have no intention of stemming the tide of illegal immigrants, because to do so, would mean corporations might have to pay higher wages.

I found it particularly galling when President Bush constantly said that the USA needed a guest worker program, so that employers could get people to do jobs Americans will not do. The truth was that he wanted a guest worker program that would afford his corporate farming friends the opportunity to hire workers at a poverty wage and provide no benefits. If a corporate farmer ran an ad saying he would pay $20 to $25 an hour for pickers, believe me, the American workers would be eager to sign on.

Having lived in California for 17 years, I always found it interesting to ride by huge vegetable fields and see the Mexican workers toiling away in the hot sun for a few dollars an hour, while on the hill above the fields would be a huge house where the owner lived in resplendent luxury. One man's luxury is usually built on the backs of hundreds, if not thousands, of people who toil in obscurity in the fields of dismay, the factories of misery or the small office cubicles of consternation that are the modern day sweat shops of despair.

American companies are now exporting this attitude of corporate slavery all over the world . In countries where worker protections are more stringent, American companies are covertly and overtly attempting to get politicians elected who will change laws so that workers can receive the same level of protection as their American counter-parts, which is almost no protection at all. The U.S. led World Bank and International Monetary Fund are constantly urging countries to do away with labour regulations in order to let the "marketplace work its magic." In other words, make it possible for corporations to exploit labour to maximize profit.

In Canada, where immigration is tightly controlled, and illegal hiring carries heavy penalties, the salaries of working men and women are higher. Canada has one of the highest rates of immigrants with higher educations in the world, and they are now attempting to attract more trades people by changing the immigrant criteria. My wife was a contractor and knew personally how difficult it was to find skilled trades people. With construction trades people making from $25 to $110 an hour, you often run into individuals with Master's degrees who have elected to change careers.

FIGHTING FOR JUSTICE

In army basic training, as I struggled to complete a ten mile hike with 60 pounds of gear on my back and an increasingly heavy M-16 rifle in my right hand, my sergeant came up beside me, reached over and took the gun out of my hand. Holding my gun in his right hand, as we continued to jog through the bush, he reached with his left hand and removed my backpack and shovel. With his own backpack already weighing him down, he gladly accepted the burden of helping me. He smiled and said, "Frye, we don't get much money, we don't get much thanks, but we belong to the best damn labour union in the world, the poor enlisted grunts of the U.S. Army, and as long as we look out for each other we can get through this." At around 5 feet 6 inches and about 140 pounds, he was not a very imposing figure, but that day, to me, he was a giant. America is filled with those who live in poverty-infested hopelessness. If only more people were like Sergeant Boxley, and would reach out with a helping hand to relieve the heavy burdens borne by those who toil in quiet desperation, the country could emerge from the darkness of despair and hopelessness into the bright sunshine of hope.

Perhaps a quote from famous defence attorney, Clarence Darrow, best sums up what I have tried to say in this chapter: "With all their faults, trade unions have done more for humanity than any other organization that ever existed and that includes the church."

CHAPTER 6
IF IT IS SUCH A NOBLE CAUSE,
HERE IS MY WEAPON, YOU GO AND FIGHT

The USA ranks 37th in the world in the availability of health care. Americans spend twice as much as residents of other developed countries on healthcare, but get lower quality, less efficiency and have the least equitable system in the entire world. Yet, the American public gets livid when they hear the word socialized medicine. They have been conditioned by the Republican right-wing politicians, who are insurance company lap dogs, to actually believe that the profit motive makes health care better in the USA.

Let me share a personal story about health care in Canada, where everyone is afforded quality health care, regardless of ability to pay. I recently talked with an old friend of mine from New York. We had just reconnected after 30 years. When I asked him how his wife was doing, he recounted the story of her battle with cancer and how they had re-mortgaged their house, and he was forced to take a second job and delay retirement to cover the medical expenses that were incurred after he reached the maximum on his medical insurance policy.

I did not have the heart to share with him what I am about to share here, but I have mentioned socialized medicine, and how Americans are brainwashed into believing there is something evil about it., so I want to share with my readers a story about Canadian health care and what it is like to live in a society that is genuinely compassionate and promises that all its citizens will have equal access to the best medical care possible at no cost.

In 2006, on New Year's Eve, I had my second stroke after immigrating to Canada. My wife helped me to the car, and we made a quick trip to the hospital. I must admit that I was scared. We got to the hospital and the parking lot was dark and foreboding. It was midnight. We go through the automatic doors, and the emergency room nurse says, "oh, it looks like you are in distress, sir. Let me help you."

She puts me in a wheelchair, asks about what is wrong, and within 30 seconds a doctor is on the scene as I am being placed on a gurney.

I watch my wife go over to a big oak desk, and I am peering through white curtains, as she asks another person where she makes arrangements. I hear the person say, "what do you mean, make arrangements?

My wife responds, "don't we have to make financial arrangements?"

The nurse smiles and says, "all I need is your Care Card. This is Canada. There are no financial arrangements. Your husband is sick, and he will be taken care of no matter what it costs."

As I lay on the gurney, waiting to be whisked away for tests, I almost cried. I remembered my dad having to put up $80,000 in order for my mother to receive a life-saving operation in America, and how he ultimately went through 1.2 million dollars to keep her alive for 7 years. I remembered all the people I knew over the years who had borrowed money or lost homes and businesses to pay for medical care. I thought to myself that Canadians had no idea how lucky they were. To those of us not born into this system, this was a miracle.

When I relate this story to Americans, I am often called a liar. They actually cannot believe that such a system exists. And those who do believe it, come up with outlandish claims that they have heard on television or read in the newspaper from the right-wingers who have never seen a corporation they did not love. One of the favourites is there is a long wait for health care in Canada, which is one of the most outlandish of all the lies perpetrated by those who are lackeys for the health insurance companies that have an iron grip on the way health care is delivered in a country that thinks the profit motive makes everything better. If there is an emergency, there is never a wait to see a doctor or receive a life-saving operation.

Even Obama's Affordable Health Care Act is nothing more than a boondoggle for the insurance companies who will be handed another 30 million customers. To make health care truly affordable, it should be funded completely by the government like it is in the rest of the civilized world. Obama, fearful of the insurance industry tycoons and ever mindful of how the Republicans destroyed Clinton's attempt at providing universal coverage, never even considered doing what was really necessary – joining the rest of the world in eliminating health insurance companies that are more interested in profits than patient welfare.

FIGHTING FOR JUSTICE

Of the 23 countries that rank ahead of the USA in life expectancy, every one of them has free health care for its citizens, but the USA doggedly sticks to its class-conscious, so-called free enterprise approach to health care. The idea of competition is supposed to make things cheaper. Does anyone really think if an individual were to stand on the street corner with a sign saying, "I need a gall bladder operation, would surgeons please place a bid," that a bevy of doctors would be competing to provide the operation at the lowest possible cost? The supply of doctors is controlled by the American Medical Association, so that there is always a manufactured shortage that insures that doctors will receive excessive compensation; although, their compensation today pales when compared to that received by the health insurance executives who get rich by denying people benefits.

America's arcane approach to health care even has a detrimental effect on the Canadian health care system. Much of the skyrocketing cost of healthcare in Canada is directly attributable to the USA being immediately south. Canadian physicians are among the best paid in the world, because doctors in Canada have the ability to hold-up the provincial governments for higher salaries by simply threatening to skip across the border and work in the corporate operated American health care system.

The USA ranks 24th in average life expectancy. It ranks first in the compensation paid to executives and it ranks first in the disparity between the rich and poor. Poverty is an integral part of the American system that allows the haves to continue their domination of the have-nots. Without a working class there would be no leisure class; therefore, poverty is an important component in the class structure that maintains a permanent underclass that is ripe for exploitation by the rich and powerful.

Even poverty is spread to other countries by American corporate greed. Many American companies that open in Canada complain about the worker safety standards here and the high wages that they say makes Canada uncompetitive in the global economy. Just like in America, they turn to the conservatives in government for help in rolling back employee benefits and safeguards. There appears to be no shortage in any country of politicians who readily serve the interests of the rich.

Poverty is at the very core of all the problems in a country where less than 100,000 people control 80% of the wealth. Let us look at a few examples of how poverty is neglected by a society that is more interested in letting the rich get richer than in instituting a system that fairly distributes the wealth to all.

In 2007, a fire engulfed a building in New York City, killing ten people from an African immigrant family. The disaster could have been prevented had the city enforced laws against wooden stair railings, and assured the building had a proper sprinkler system. Of course, adequate fire escapes would also have been helpful. If the city had affordable housing, twenty-two people would not have been crowded in a facility for eight.

FIGHTING FOR JUSTICE

A faulty electric heater was blamed for starting the fire. Due to the high cost of utilities and no real assistance for the impoverished, it is estimated that over 25,000 fires and hundreds of deaths are caused each year due to people using unsafe methods of staying warm.

When New York's billionaire mayor, Michael Bloomberg, was asked about the tragedy, he replied the city would be handing out free batteries for fire alarms. How magnanimous of him to suggest handing out 99 cent batteries to solve the problem of poverty. Meanwhile, his rich friends on Park Avenue probably also got the free batteries along with their other preferential treatments. While the poor are living on the streets and being burned alive in substandard housing, the city put itself on the hook for $700,000,000 to assist in building a new Yankee Stadium for the billionaire owner who threatened to leave the city if he did not get his stadium. Talk about welfare? There never seems to be any outcry from the politicians when welfare is used to assist corporations and billionaires, but poor people are just freeloaders..

As the U.S. government assails Venezuela's President Hugo Chavez for his socialistic policies in an attempt to more evenly spread the wealth of his oil rich country, this hated socialist arranges to send free and subsidized heating oil to the residents of New York City, who are neglected and ignored by their own government that can always find money for bombs, bullets and tax cuts for the rich, but can never find the necessary funds to provide for the most vulnerable in the richest society in the history of the world.

FIGHTING FOR JUSTICE

America's solution to poverty is to simply ignore it, or in some cases make it a crime. Apparently, this disregard for humanity even extends to the healthcare industry. In Los Angeles, there have been many documented cases of the poor being taken from hospitals and dumped on Skid Row. In one such case, a patient from a Hollywood Hospital fell out of the back of an ambulance and the driver just left with him lying in the street. To add insult to injury, the man was a paraplegic and was forced to crawl onto the sidewalk until other homeless people called another ambulance.

The so-called non-profit Kaiser Permanente Health Care Organization was caught on videotape dropping off a 62-year-old patient on Skid Row in her hospital gown. These are not just isolated incidents. They are occurring all over America as the for-profit healthcare system continues to ignore the needs of patients who do not have insurance, and Obama's health care law is just a continuation of this greed based approach.

What is the solution to the homeless situation? Many cities are attacking the problem by reducing the visibility of the homeless. Laws against sleeping on sidewalks and in doorways or in makeshift camps have, in effect, made being homeless a crime. Some cities are even transporting the homeless outside the city limits and dumping them like hospitals dump indigent patients.

As big business begins to buy up more property in the inner city, the police have become the storm troopers for capitalism as they arrest, harass and detain the homeless to gentrify the areas and make the environments more conducive for their corporate masters.

All the money spent on George W. Bush's war for oil in Iraq could have eliminated homelessness in America in a few short years with massive public shelter building projects, which would have also spurred the economy to unprecedented heights. Yet, the government would rather spend money to bomb and strafe a foreign land so the defence contractors can make billions supplying the weapons to reduce a country to a pile of rubble. Then, other companies like Halliburton, are awarded huge contracts to rebuild what other corporate bottom feeders have been paid to destroy. Where are all the Jesus-loving Christians while this is going on? They are all waving the flag and shouting the righteousness of American values. Meanwhile, they never think about how all that money could go to a cause that their beloved Jesus would obviously prefer over killing, feeding the hungry and sheltering the homeless.

I corresponded by e-mail with a soldier in Iraq right after the invasion. I tried to explain to him how the government was representing the rich and powerful and using him to enrich greedy corporations. I pointed out to him that his own commander and chief, George W. Bush had avoided service in Vietnam by hiding in the National Guard, and that while he thought that he was fighting for freedom, the sons and daughters of the President, the Cabinet, Congresspersons and Senators were enjoying lives of privilege with no fear of having to die in a needless war. For many months, we continued to correspond as I tried to explain to him another military fiasco called the Vietnam War. Yet, years of intense patriotic conditioning prevented him from seeing through the dark veil of lies and deceit that keeps so many young people imprisoned to patriotic servitude.

Somehow, we got on the subject of taxes and income distribution. I tried to illustrate to him how the rich were treated favourably by a tax structure that was not truly progressive, and let them keep an excessive amount of their income while the middle class was expected to pay the freight for both the poor and wealthy. I tried to explain to him that he was fighting for freedom, but those who sent him out to die, expected him to do it on poverty wages. It seemed to dawn on him that there was a great income disparity, not only in the general population, but in the military population as well.

When I asked him how much he was being paid a year to defend freedom, he said his basic pay was around $16,000. (This was 2003.) I did a web search on military pay and explained to him that the generals who sit in safe compounds away from the fighting were being paid around $170,000 a year. Then, I told him that the Congress that voted on his low military compensation paid themselves $165,000 a year with benefits even more lavish than the generals got. I asked him to tell me how many generals and colonels had been killed in the war since he had been there, and then to compare that to the number of privates and corporals who had been killed. Suddenly, I think it began to dawn on him that his life was considered less valuable than those of a higher socio-economic class than he was. Even the military, which ballyhoos its great equality, has definite class distinctions that are to never be breeched.

When I asked him what his father and mother did, he replied that his mother was a homemaker, and that his father worked in a factory. I asked him what his father made, and he replied that it was around $28,000 a year. Again, I did some on-line research and explained to him that executives who run corporations like the one for whom his dad toils received salary increases of around 300% in the last 15 years. If his dad and other factory workers had received the same increases, his father and those like him would be earning an average of $110,000 a year in 2003.

I went on to explain to him how the U.S. government was using terrorism to fight terrorism by incarcerating people in sub-human conditions, engaging in torture and using things like cluster bombs in a country they accused of hoarding weapons of mass destruction. In other words, weapons of mass destruction in the hands of America are not weapons of mass destruction; they just represent the justified use of military force. Then I brought up a few examples of how America supported terrorism when it was to America's advantage, like the crushing of the socialist revolution in Chile that occurred on 9/11/1973 and resulted in even more deaths than the American 9/11 disaster.

I used several other examples of how America supported terrorists when it served its interests, but since he was Hispanic, one case seemed of particular interest to him. I used the example Luis Posada

Carriles, a man notorious for his suspected 1976 mid-air bombing of a Cuban airliner that killed 73 people. He is also rumoured to have been involved in the bombing of a Havana hotel and to have been on the CIA payroll. Then, he was arrested in Panama for attempting to assassinate Fidel Castro. The Bush Administration vehemently lobbied for his pardon, and eventually the Panama government caved in. Immediately upon his release, he skipped across the American border and was arrested for illegal immigration. Again, the Bush Administration came to his rescue when, after his arrest, Cuba and Venezuela asked that he be extradited to stand trial for his numerous criminal acts. The judge refused to extradite him, due to the Bush Administration's claim that he might be tortured. This seemed to be the height of hypocrisy from a country that used water boarding, sleep deprivation and noise excruciation to torture prisoners at Abu Ghraib and Guantanamo Bay.

It was not long until this young man had many of his friends talking to me. I am proud to say that when his tour of duty was over, he refused to reenlist, went to university and is now a teacher.

As long as poverty is ignored by a society with the ability to eliminate it almost overnight, and the tax structure rewards the rich at the expense of the poor and middle class, no American middle class or poor youths should be expected to serve in wars of conquest. If it were the children and the grandchildren of the rich and powerful who had to die, there would be no unjust wars. It is high time that the poor and middle class youths who are expected to serve the so-called cause of freedom, simply take their guns, hand them to the children of the rich and powerful, and say, "if it is such a noble cause, here is my weapon, you go and fight."

CHAPTER 7
RALPH JOHNS
AND THE MARKET STREET MAVERICKS

Most people over the age of 50 remember Martin Luther King's, "I Have a Dream Speech." However, most of us are unaware of the speech he gave on poverty and civil rights when at the height of the Vietnam War he said, "the United States government is the greatest purveyor of violence in the world." He saw through the folly of fighting wars of conquest, when the greatest battle of all needed to be fought in the heart of America to insure that all Americans had equal opportunity and equal rights under the law. He was dismayed by a system that used the disenfranchised and poor to fight wars while the children of the wealthy and privileged were given a pass.

This battle for equality has been long and arduous. It continues today, as race is no longer the most common barrier to upward mobility. Today, it is not just race, although African-Americans and Hispanics are disproportionably poor, but poverty itself that leads to discrimination. The poor are kept poor by a system that refuses to reward those who do the physical labour in society.

As a child in the southern USA, I was brought up on a steady diet of white superiority. I can remember from an early age being taught that segregation was permissible, because even the Bible said that God had sent the Blacks to Africa as the tribe of Ham. All my relatives had been reared with prejudices. In later life, it was easy to judge my relatives for their prejudices, and I often did, but today, I can look back and see that they, too, were victims, just like African Americans. They were victims of a society that had made segregation and white superiority the very fabric of its culture. From one generation to another, hatred for African Americans had been passed on like a family heirloom.

While I was attending elementary and secondary schools in the south, there was a strict separation of races. I never sat beside an African American in a classroom until university, because they were relegated to an old, dilapidated, rundown building in the poorest section of town, while I went to a bright, well-equipped, spotlessly clean school in the white part of town. As a young child, I never questioned this segregation as I was told that they got what they had, because they did not know how to behave in a nice school and would just tear it up. Anyway, they were not as smart as white people, and did not really need an education for the menial jobs they would be doing. As a six or seven year old child, you begin to form opinions based upon what you are told by adults.

It is easy to understand why religious leaders want to get children started in Sunday school at an early age. They know, just like the tobacco companies, that the key to indoctrination is getting young children so they can control and manipulate their minds before they have an opportunity to develop cognitive skills and be more discerning in what they accept as fact. I can even recall attending churches where the ministers preached against integration, because, according to them, God was the one who originally separated the races.

FIGHTING FOR JUSTICE

Martin Luther King was a pariah to most white southerners in the small town where I lived, because he did not know his place. I remember one minister who even said he was a representative of the devil and a communist, which made him an abomination in the eyes of God.

Fortunately, as a child, I had a grandmother, who, though prejudiced in her own way against African Americans because of her heritage, still had that spark deep down inside that said something was not right about the way they were treated. I can remember watching the news with her one night when Rosa Parks refusal to give up her seat to a white man in Montgomery, Alabama was the top story. She turned to me and said, "that woman is right Wayne. Just because she is coloured, don't mean she should give up her seat to a white man. She paid to ride, too."

That night is indelibly stamped in my conscience, as it was the first time I saw her question what she had been taught all her life. I had seen her reach out with the hand of compassion to African Americans with whom she came into contact over the years. She had allowed me to play with an African American child whose father came to work at her home. She even permitted me to go home with him and spend the day, but that night I saw a woman in her 60's who had confronted her heritage head-on, and finally vocalized what had been beneath the surface for so long. She had been a victim of her environment, and finally opened up with what she had kept bottled up in her for over 60 years in a society that ostracized those who dared question the way things were.

FIGHTING FOR JUSTICE

I mention these episodes, because I think it is important before discussing the next unsung heroes to have some background into the area and era in which I was a child, and to understand that the North Carolina in which I was reared was a much different place than it is today.

Ralph Johns was born in New Castle, Pennsylvania, probably around 1915, although, I have never been able to pinpoint the exact date. I should also add that he was white, which will be important later on. He was a bit player in the movies in the 1930's, and for a while, a stand-in and double for one of the all-time great movie tough-guys and later Havana casino owner, George Raft. After being discharged from the army in 1944, he settled in Greensboro, North Carolina and opened a clothing store on Market Street.

At the time, African Americans were not excluded from white-owned clothing stores, but they were not welcomed either. However, Johns let it be known that he was interested in serving the African American community. His store became very popular among students from the all-black North Carolina A & T University, which meant it became unpopular with the whites; consequently, his business's survival was at stake since he openly solicited black customers.

Johns became the first white member of the local NAACP (National Association for the Advancement of Coloured People), and very quickly incurred the wrath of many whites, and particularly the Ku Klux Klan, which at the time, had a fairly strong presence in Greensboro. Never one to back down from a confrontation, Johns refused to be intimidated by any individual or group.

Before continuing with the story, let me once again provide you a little background on my childhood, so the younger readers, particularly in Canada, can understand what the environment of the southern United States was at that time. As a child, I never questioned why no African Americans attended my school. I did not give serious thought to never seeing an African American in a managerial position. When I went into the dime store to buy a sack of popcorn, and walked over to the water fountain for a drink, I thought there was nothing peculiar about seeing two water fountains side by side. One was spotlessly clean and said, "Whites Only." The other was dirty and said "Coloured Only," as did the bathrooms.

I never questioned why I would go out to a restaurant for dinner with my mom and dad, and there would be no African-Americans in the place. After all, why should I expect them to be in restaurants when they were not even permitted to attend the same school as I did? For a white child, it seemed normal to me that restaurants in town were for whites only, just like the schools. I was probably 7 or 8 years old before I noticed that African-Americans had to go to the back kitchen door of the restaurant and pick up their food to take home or eat outside. Ironically, the cooks in the restaurants were usually African-American as were the dishwashers and other menial labourers. They could work at menial jobs and serve white people, but they could not eat in the same restaurants where they worked out of sight and out of mind.

FIGHTING FOR JUSTICE

I began to question this practice at a young age, but as a member of the favoured class, I did not bring it up with anyone other than my most trusted confidant, my grandmother. Fearing how my family might react to my questioning of segregation, I assiduously avoided the subject.

During this period, the same type of environment was prevalent in the nearby city of Greensboro. It was in this city that Ralph Johns fought his lonely battle to integrate the restaurants, schools and other public facilities. He met with opposition from influential political figures, and particularly from the powerful local chapter of the Ku Klux Klan, which often severely punished any white person who dared lend assistance to the fledgling civil rights movement. White economic boycotts of his store, threats to harm him and ostracism by friends and neighbours never deterred him from fighting his lonely battle against a government that sanctioned segregation in order to keep order. His commitment to justice and fair play has gone largely unnoticed by a nation that makes heroes out of the wrong people.

Johns is thought to have encouraged the students to challenge segregation and to have tipped off the press about the first mass sit-in demonstration of the civil rights movement which took place at the Woolworth's lunch counter in downtown Greensboro on Market Street. On February 1, 1960, African-American North Carolina A & T students, Ezell Blair, Jr., David Richmond, Joseph McNeil and Franklin McCain sat down at a lunch counter in the Woolworth's Dime Store. As they sat at the lunch counter, they were continuously refused service, as it was the policy at the time in all white owned restaurants that African Americans could not be served on premises.

In 1964, I was clandestinely dating an African-American high school student in Greensboro. One day, her brother asked me if I wanted to buy some clothes at a discount. Needing some nice threads, as we called them in those days, I said, "sure." He told me that he could get me a 10% discount at the clothing store where he worked. That was the day I met Ralph Johns. From that day on, for about one year, before going off to university, I made it a point to frequent his store regularly, not to buy clothes, but to discuss the civil rights movement with him. I was fascinated and enthralled by his commitment to equality for all Americans, and heard many tales of how the government was harassing him for his involvement with the civil rights movement. He was called a communist by a variety of government agencies and was under frequent surveillance. All this directed at a poor clothing store proprietor, who was committed to seeing that the U.S. Constitution should apply to all citizens.

After leaving for university and the military, I only saw him on a few occasions in the late 1960's and early 1970's. In the late 1960's, he was actually somewhat recognized for his commitment to civil rights when he was appointed an organizer for the Guilford County Office of Economic Opportunity. However, his fiery manner soon got him in trouble, when he accused the agency of talking about doing something for the poor, but never really doing anything. His intense commitment to the civil rights movement also caused strains in his marriage, which eventually led to divorce. His clothing store fell on hard times, when even the African-Americans abandoned his establishment for the more trendy uptown stores that were now welcoming African-American customers. Still boycotted by most whites, he eventually closed-up. He returned to Hollywood, where he tried to resume his movie career with very little success. In 1977, he returned to Greensboro to help his second wife launch a tabloid newspaper.

I last saw him in 1971, and was deeply moved when he lamented to me that he felt the movement to which he had been so committed just seemed to have forgotten him. I smiled at Ralph and assured him that I would never forget him, because he had opened a young man's eyes to the possibilities of a world where all people are genuinely created equal, and above all, guaranteed equal opportunity. He left Greensboro again a few years later and returned to Los Angeles to work at a newspaper. He died there in 1996, still a forgotten hero in the battle for civil rights.

In the summer of 2001, my wife and I visited North Carolina to see my ailing father. Her interest in antibellum architecture led to a Greensboro visit. While there, I had her meander down Market Street with me, which, for the most part, had become a string of antique stores. I pointed out to her the storefront where I had listened intently to the musings of Ralph Johns. I suggested to her that it might be interesting to visit the famous Woolworth's store, where the first American sit-in took place. Not being able to find it, we entered an old Ella Stone Department Store building that had been turned into a huge antique gallery. We asked a woman of about 70, who was behind the counter, where was the old Woolworth's store that was the site of the famous sit-ins. She replied, "oh, you mean the place where the coloureds took over."

After getting directions, on the way out the door, I said to my wife. "Thank goodness, most of the younger people in the south do not think that way anymore, but what you just heard is an example of the way people thought when I was young. Thank goodness for Ralph Johns and the Market Street mavericks."

CHAPTER 8
THERE AIN'T A DIME'S WORTH
OF DIFFERENCE

After the many foreign policy fiascos and the downright incompetence of the Bush Administration, many people looked back on the Clinton presidency with great nostalgia. No doubt, George Bush one day will be mentioned in history books as one of America's worst Presidents. Whether Democrat or Republican, no Presidents, other than Franklin Roosevelt and Teddy Roosevelt have ever been a friend of the working people in America. And even those two had their limitations when it came to helping those on the lower rungs of the socio-economic ladder.

No doubt, Clinton's level of competence far exceeded that of the "boob from Texas." Of course, comparing Clinton to Bush is like comparing a Rolls Royce to a go-cart. Yet, if you look at Clinton's record, he was no real friend of the working person either. If you made a lot of money in the stock market in those days, as I did, you might look back on the Clinton era with fondness. Of course, what I made I wound up losing the first few months Bush was in office, and then really took a bath in the final years of the Bush march to the ultimate economic meltdown.

Clinton knew that the secret to winning elections for the Democrats was to move from liberalism to conservatism. The American people are, outside of the Muslim countries, the most conservative electorate in the world. God is just as much a part of American politics, as Allah is a part of Middle Eastern politics.

FIGHTING FOR JUSTICE

Clinton is the one who pushed through NAFTA, which has deflated working people's wages since it was passed, and has led to a mass exodus of manufacturing jobs to Mexico. When the first edition of this book was going to press, it was rumoured that China was negotiating with Mexican authorities to build a huge car manufacturing plant in Mexico, so it could avoid a 25% tariff by exporting them to the USA from Mexico, a member of NAFTA, rather than from China. Although negotiations are still on-going, it appears that this, if it finally comes to fruition, will just be another example of American workers having to suffer as a result of NAFTA, which makes free trade nothing more than an excuse to suppress American working people's wages.

Clinton also presided over the dismantling of the welfare program, catering to conservatives, so he could be re-elected in 1996. Even the draconian, fascist Patriotic Act was already in rough draft form by the end of the Clinton Administration. As for big business, the mergers and the out-sourcing of jobs, although only a trickle compared to Bush's flood, never met any resistance from the business-loving Clinton Administration.

While catering to big business, Clinton cut programs aimed at the underprivileged. He had no spine for a real fight with the Republican fascists in Congress, caving in on every nomination he made to the Supreme Court and cabinet posts. If the Republican Congress squawked too much, he simply withdrew the nomination. In most cases, he nominated middle of the road people or conservatives in order to assure his nominees would be approved. In effect, it was still the Republicans who were controlling the Executive Branch of the government, even though they had lost the Presidency, much as they wound up doing under Obama, who also constantly caved into them. Most people are not astute enough to realize that the only reason Clinton beat Bush in 1992, was that Ross Perot tilted the election by siphoning off so many Republican voters. As mentioned previously, Americans, after Muslims, are the most conservative voters in the world, so by having two conservative candidates, it was possible for Clinton to squeak into office. Obama simply got elected, because Americans were literally fed-up with 8 years of having an idiot in the White House. Of course, the fact that an exceedingly articulate Obama was going up against an inarticulate John McCain, who was proclaimed a hero, even by Obama, for dropping bombs on women and children from 80,000 feet during the Vietnam War, made the choice rather easy.

I am sure many of my liberal friends will be offended by my previous comments about Clinton, but there was a pattern of pampering big business long before he became President. As governor of Arkansas, he catered to the clear cutting forest giant Weyerhaeuser, when he lost an election after they backed his opponent. He is rumoured to have walked into the Weyerhaeuser corporate office after the election and said, "sorry about the trouble I caused you, but when I get elected governor in two years, I will make amends." (At the time, Arkansas elected their governor every two years.) He also made sure that Tyson Foods was able to continue its exploitation of cheap labour in a state notorious for lax environmental laws and poor business regulation.

Most of Clinton's campaigns in Arkansas were financed by big business. One billionaire, Joseph Stephens, constantly loaned or donated huge amounts of money to the Clinton campaigns. He was one of the biggest contributors to his 1992 Presidential campaign. Therefore, it should be no surprise that only a few months after being elected, Clinton turned to Wall Street for his economic advisers.

The ultimate betrayal of working people was the Clinton Administration's inability to try and get a single payer health plan passed that would make America like every other civilized country in the world by providing its citizens with free healthcare. Unwilling to fight the health insurance industry, Hillary came up with a hodgepodge of ideas that made the corporate insurance giants the beneficiaries of any plan that would pass. She, like the rest of the government employees, did not have to worry about health insurance, because there health plans were all paid for by the American taxpayers, while the taxpayers themselves were not entitled to the same treatment. As long as the USA has a for-profit healthcare system, millions of Americans will continue to suffer from the greatest sickness of all, corporate greed.

It was during the Clinton Presidency that the ultimate operative of the right wing, Congressman Newt Gingrich, saw that the Clintons were easy prey. He effectively neutralized them for six years when he engineered the infamous "Contract with America" that brought the Republicans into control of both Houses of Congress from 1994 to 2006. Congressional Republican rule assured that Bill Clinton would not be allowed to help working people in America, even if he wanted to do so.

The appointment of George Bush as President in 2000 gave the Republicans control of the Legislative Branch and the Executive Branch of government. Then, with Bush's Supreme Court appointments, they even gained control of the judiciary branch. This feat assured the solidification of corporate domination of America. Thanks to the conservative majority on the court, the infamous Citizens United Supreme Court Ruling has guaranteed the corporations and the rich the intrinsic right to simply buy elections in an even more blatant manor. All restraints have been removed now, so that there are no controls whatsoever on how the rich and powerful can completely control the electoral process through massive spending that guarantees the gullible public will be persuaded to vote against their own interests.

As usual, Americans are unable to understand how their own government functions. They do not realize that by electing a conservative President, they assure that the Supreme Court appointments he or she makes will also swing to the right. The Supreme Court makes crucial decisions on the laws that affect every American. These judges are appointed for life, so the President may go, but these people may stay for 20, 30, 40 or even 50 years. They have a much more profound effect on America than the President does. Today, this is the august body that is edging ever closer to telling women they have no control over their own bodies, that the government has a right to spy on its own citizens, that it is permissible to torture prisoners, that the government has a right to detain people indefinitely it considers a threat to the state, that corporations should be shielded from abusive lawsuits, that incompetent doctors should be shielded from paying excessive damages when a patient is treated improperly and that workers have no inherent right to unionize.

It was a liberal Supreme Court, put in place initially by Franklin Roosevelt, which in the 1940's and 1950's ushered in an era of the court siding with the working people of America. This led to an unprecedented expansion of a middle class in the USA that made it possible for the average person to get just a small slice of that thing called the American dream. This same court lowered the curtain on segregation with the famous *Brown vs. the Board of Education* decision in 1954 that said separate but equal facilities were inherently unequal by the very nature of being separate. Today's nine member Supreme Court has a five person majority appointed by Republicans that is doing everything possible to roll back all the gains of the last 50 years.

With the election of 2006, Americans thought they had a chance to change things when both houses of Congress were taken over by the Democrats, but after only a few months, it became apparent that the Democrats had no stomach for taking on a Republican President or big business. It was not long until

Congress's approval ratings lagged far behind those of George W. Bush, the second most unpopular President in United States history. Then, when Obama got a majority in both houses of Congress in the 2008 election, he was still hampered by a Senate that required 60 votes to pass any major legislation. So, with only 59 Democrats, he simply could not get anything worthwhile done. Stalemate aids the status-quo, so once again, the rich and powerful come out on top.

Democrats and Republicans are only labels for two parties that con the American people into thinking they have their best interests in mind, anyway. Like the capitalistic, corporate, corrupt masters of greed that they serve, their only interest is what they can get for themselves. Why did these bastions of probity sit idly by while the U.S. Justice Department freed a known Mexican drug smuggler in order to have him testify against two border patrol agents who had the nerve to try and enforce American immigration laws?

Ignacio Ramos and Jose Campion were two border control agents who shot a fleeing Mexico drug smuggler who was in the USA illegally. U.S. Attorney for the Western District of Texas, Johnny Sutton, a Bush appointee, decided that these agents acted illegally by going after a known criminal who had been deported from America several times for drug smuggling. While the country has millions of illegal aliens crossing the Mexican border every year, Sutton decides to give immunity to a drug smuggler for his testimony against two agents who were actually doing their jobs. The trouble is, the better these men do their jobs, the fewer illegal workers available to depress American wages.

While the drug smuggler walked, and, no doubt, is still slipping across the border to deliver illegal drugs in a society that has been in a so-called war on drugs for years, two border patrol agents got 12 years in prison for doing their jobs. This sentence was a clear message to the U.S. Border Patrol that stringent enforcement of immigration laws is a detriment to big business, and will not be tolerated by a government intent on assuring that corporate American has a steady supply of immigrant labour to exploit. This exploitation requires an open border with Mexico for the free-flow of cheap labour to keep American workers from demanding higher wages and more benefits.

Why do both parties, Republican and Democratic, refuse to stand up to big business in defence of the working people of America? The answer is extremely simple. The government leaders, with few exceptions, are all members of the wealthy class. The 100 member Senate has 98 millionaires. Even the non-millionaires who are elected, do not take long to join the ranks of the wealthy, based on a base salary of approximately $170,000 a year, lavish perks, expense accounts and a bevy of freebees from the corporate lobbyists. At one time, the American taxpayers even subsidized the haircuts of members of Congress, who were only required to pay $1.50 for a haircut. These are the same people who deny universal healthcare to the American people, but make sure they get the best health coverage available for free or at a reduced rate.

FIGHTING FOR JUSTICE

It is clear that whichever party is elected, the American government will never address the needs of the average person. In fact, the very idea of the two party system is to simply give the American voter an illusion of democracy. Several times in U.S. elections, the winner of the popular vote did not become President, because of the arcane system of assigning a number of electoral votes based on each state's population. This most recently occurred in 2000, when George Bush lost the election by over one million votes, but won the Presidency simply because he received more electoral votes. In a democracy, the person with the most votes would win; therefore, by definition, America is not a democracy.

Third or fourth party candidates are effectively frozen out of the system. Throughout American history, there have been many valiant efforts by third parties to mount a challenge to this exclusionary system that perpetuates the control of the wealthy and powerful while ignoring the real needs of the people. Let us look at a few examples of people who tried to break the two party monopolies.

Almost all American Presidents have been members of the Fraternal Order of Masons, and for that reason, in 1832; the Anti-Masonic Party actually fielded a candidate, William Wirt, for President, who won 7 electoral votes. In 1848, the Free Soil Party nominated former President Martin Van Buren as its candidate in New York, thereby splitting the vote in New York and causing the election of Zachary Taylor in a close race. In 1860, there was a four party race for the White House when the Democrats broke into two parties and the Constitutional Party fielded a candidate against the Republicans and Democrats. This led to the election of a President who still holds the record for being elected with the smallest percentage of the popular vote. Abraham Lincoln became President with only 39% of the popular vote. In 1892, the Populist Party won 22 electoral votes, but in 1912, the most successful third party race in history was run by former President Teddy Roosevelt as the standard bearer for the Bull Moose Party. He actually finished ahead of Republican incumbent William Howard Taft, who not only holds the record for the heaviest President in history (300 pounds), but also has the distinction of being the only incumbent President seeking re-election to finish third. Woodrow Wilson won the Presidency with 42% of the vote. This was also the first year that noted socialist, Eugene V. Debs, ran for President, receiving 6% of the vote. Debs was eventually jailed for opposing the World War I draft by encouraging men to ignore their draft notices since it appeared the poor were being called up while the rich were getting a pass, and he is the only man to ever run for President while incarcerated. His radical views on redistributing wealth led to a lifetime of jail sentences and harassment by a government that saw him as a threat to capitalism.

In 1948, Strom Thurmond ran on the segregationist Dixiecrat ticket, splitting the Democratic vote and winning 39 electoral votes, all from the southern states. Twenty years later in 1968, another southerner, George Corley Wallace, governor of Alabama, received more electoral votes than any third party candidate in history has, when he received 46 electoral votes, all from the south.

FIGHTING FOR JUSTICE

If it were not for Ross Perot, the Republican Party would have won every election from 1980 to 2008. The eccentric billionaire, who made most of his money off government contracts, mounted one of the best third party runs in history, and received 19% of the votes in 1992, taking most of his support from disaffected Republicans; thereby, assuring that Bill Clinton would win the Presidency with only 43% of the popular vote.

Of course, everyone is familiar with the 2000 election of George Bush because of Green Party candidate, Ralph Nader, who received 19,000 votes in Florida, almost all coming from Democrats who would have voted for Al Gore. As a result, Bush won the state by less than 600 votes, when the Republican appointed majority on the U.S. Supreme Court (5-4) refused a recount of the Florida votes due to irregularities that apparently denied a vast number of African-Americans the opportunity to cast a ballot. (Bush, like three other Presidents before him, actually lost the popular vote.) This was one of the few third party attempts that had a profound effect on America. Unfortunately the effect was negative, as the nation wound up with an elitist, religious zealot in the White House who solidified the corporate hold on America, instituted a huge tax cut for the wealthy to further widen the gap between the haves and have-nots, ignored the plight of the middle class and embarked on an arrogant foreign policy that led to the deaths of hundreds of thousands of innocent men, women and children, while turning America and its military into one of the most hated entities on earth. Then, in the 2004 election, irregularities in the Ohio vote were just ignored, as the Democrats knew that the

5-4 Republican majority on the Supreme Court would ignore the obvious voter fraud, and the result would have been in Bush's favour again.

Winning elections is not really an option for third parties. All they can hope to do is bring certain issues before the American public, so they will at least get a hearing.

One needs to look back at the aforementioned George Corley Wallace, who vowed in the early 1960's, "segregation today, segregation tomorrow, segregation forever," to get a real understanding of what the American two party system is all about. Although, at one time an avowed racist, toward the end of his life, Wallace made it a point to go to African-American churches in his wheel chair to admit he had been wrong. In his later terms as governor of Alabama, he instituted many programs aimed at lending assistance to the Black Alabamians whom he had often neglected in previous terms as governor just to be elected in a state that was known for its racist philosophy.

When he ran for President twice on a third party ticket, he drew huge crowds all over America with his populist appeals. He knew that he could only be a spoiler, not a winner, and all he hoped for was an election where the two major candidates would not have enough electoral votes to be elected, and with his few electoral votes, he could swing the election by getting some concessions in order to assign his electors to one of the candidates. He wound up with 13.5% of the vote, mostly from the deep south.

FIGHTING FOR JUSTICE

Wallace brought many audiences, even in the northern states, to their feet with several favourite lines attacking the status-quo and the two party system that kept America in its grip. A highly educated man, with a law degree, he was a long-time judge who was a master of the English language, but he was famous for using his southern accent and plain language to arouse his audiences, which were made up, primarily, of working people. One of his most famous lines was in reference to the United States Congress, the President, the Cabinet members and the government bureaucrats who were running the country while reaping huge salaries and benefits. He said, "them big boys up in Washington ain't nothing special. They put their britches (pants) on one leg at a time, just like the rest of us."

Although an obvious racist at the time, his "common-man touch," won him great plaudits from those who saw the typical Washington politician as simply out of touch with the typical American's problems. To many Americans, especially southerners, he represented what was lacking in other politicians.

In the 1968 campaign for President, frustrated at not being afforded equal opportunities with the two parties that control the American political agenda, he realized that there was no hope for third parties in a corrupt system that owed its allegiance to the corporate power brokers that controlled the political purse strings. At almost every campaign function, he uttered these immortal words, "when it comes to the Democratic Party and the Republican Party, they ain't a dime's worth of difference between 'um."

CHAPTER 9
IF ONLY THERE WERE MORE LIKE HIM

The defining moment in my development of a social conscience came about while I was in the military. I received transfer orders to serve in a clandestine specialized intelligence unit. As mentioned in a previous chapter, when I went to the Pentagon to work for the Army Chief of Staff for Intelligence, reviewing top-secret documents and engaging in nefarious activities to stifle dissent at home and abroad, I was exposed to the truth about America. This truth led to questioning everything I had been taught as a child.

During this period of my life, the pursuit of fairness and justice for the less fortunate in a world that is rife with intolerance and lack of compassion became of paramount importance. Unfortunately, compassion and commitment to justice comes at a very high price, as we have seen from the previous examples in this book. In America, those who fight the establishment pay an extremely high price for doing so.

Many people have accused me of supporting a system of government-institutionalized equality. Nothing could be further from the truth. What I have always envisioned is a system that guarantees equality of opportunity. For example, why should the children of the wealthy and powerful get an inside track on success just because they have the good fortunate to be born to the right parents? Why should the children of wealthy parents be given the best medical care while the children of the poor are carted off to ghetto hospitals? Why should the children of the wealthy be afforded the opportunity to attend Harvard just because their parents can afford it? Being born with a silver spun in your mouth should not be the ticket to success that it is in the USA.

Karl Marx and Frederick Engels in *The Communist Manifesto* never envisioned an equal society. What they wanted was an equal opportunity society. Marx stated, "once the aim of the proletariat movement, the abolition of classes, has been attained, the power of the state, which serves to keep the great majority of workers under the yoke of a small exploiting minority, disappears, and the functions of government are transformed into simple administrative functions." Marx sought to change government from the servant of the moneyed oligarchy to the servant of the masses who have to meekly beg for the crumbs they are thrown.

I have always been amazed at how Americans constantly attack communism, but most Americans have never even taken the time to read *The Communist Manifesto*. If they had done so, rather than swallowing American government propaganda, they would have realized that the Soviet Union and China were never communist countries, they were simply one party dictatorships that hid under the guise of communist doctrine to manipulate their own people, just as the USA manipulates its citizens into thinking they have a two party system that affords the populace an opportunity to participate in democracy. The truth is simply that America, like the aforementioned countries that were vilified for years during the Cold War, only exudes a facade of democracy while resting the real power, not in the electorate, but the wealthy barons of greed who know that politics, like everything else in America, comes down to money.

Engels, even more so than Marx, saw that powerful institutions and individuals could never be abolished, as the very nature of humanity necessitated a willingness on the part of the governed to submit to some authority in order to maintain social order. Without social order, men would revert to an even more primitive state that would only allow the physically powerful to exert control, just as they had during the cave dwelling period, as opposed to the wealthy, who exercise control in the modern world. Societies must have rules that protect the weak from the powerful. In America, there are no such rules. The rich have encouraged the U.S. government to allow uncontrolled immigration in order to keep working people's salaries as low as possible. Since the election of Ronald Reagan in 1980, the salaries of America's CEO's have mushroomed by 300% to 700% when adjusted for inflation. Meanwhile, the average factory worker lost around $4600 in purchasing power between 1980 and 2012. In 2012 dollars, a factory worker in America made the equivalent of $17.60 an hour in 1980. Today, that same worker earns the equivalent of $12.25. In 1965, the average CEO made 44 times what the average factory worker did. In 2012, the average CEO was making 386 times what the average factory worker did. If the minimum wage kept pace with CEO pay increases since 1960, the minimum wage in America would be $65.00 an hour today. This obscene inequity is promoted by a government dedicated to serving the rich and powerful, while turning its back on the needs of the middle class and poor. This same government likes to brag about equality in the American workplace. Where is this equality when the wealthy take the whole loaf of bread, while leaving the labourers crumbs?

For years, the U.S. government knew that car companies made defective, unsafe products, but rarely did the government act to protect the consumer. It took a book by Ralph Nader to expose the callousness of the General Motors Corporation that filled the roads of America with a product called the Corvair that was a death trap. While this was going on, the government allowed the car companies to regulate themselves. If it had been left up to the car companies, there would still be no seatbelts in automobiles today. This should be no surprise in a country where a Republican President once said, "what is good for General Motors is good for America."

The Republican party of today wants to go back to this model that allows the giant corporations to regulate themselves. Mitt Romney's famous statement that "corporations are people, too" is the actual mind-set of a party dedicated to vilifying the poor while exalting the rich whom they think deserve more and more, even if it has to come out of the pockets of those who can least afford it.

If a criminal takes a gun and shoots someone, it is murder. If a corporation makes a product that kills you, because they do not want to spend the few extra dollars to make it safe, that is just good business. The Ford Pinto needed a part that only cost a few dollars to keep it from exploding when rear-ended. Yet, the company figured it would be cheaper to settle lawsuits than to install the part.

As mentioned in a previous chapter, the U.S. government has been involved in a war on drugs for many years. While billions are spent to incarcerate drug users in corporate operated prisons and to run television ads that preach about the evils of drugs, this same government allows cigarette companies to inject nicotine into their product in order to addict people. Even the food industry uses special additives to make people crave snack foods.

During the Bush presidency, nearly 4 million manufacturing jobs were lost in America. While corporate profits soared, workers salaries went down in constant dollars. The uninsured during the Bush Presidency climbed to nearly 50,000,000, and those able to afford insurance saw their premiums go up 30% to 80% while the U.S. health care's ranking slipped to 37th in the world. Meanwhile, the profits of the HMO's and insurance companies hit the stratosphere. What was the Republican solution when Obama finally got his health care act passed? They tried to repeal it 33 times, even though they knew a Presidential veto would prevent it. Although I was terribly disappointed in the Affordable Care Act, because it still put health care in the hands of the insurance companies, at least it was a step in the right direction toward a system where health care was universal and provided by the government, rather than a corporation that had rather let people die than provide the benefits to which their policy holders were entitled.

FIGHTING FOR JUSTICE

Even after the Supreme Court ruled the bill Constitutional, 44% of the American public did not support the bill, because they feared it was a step toward that horrible evil that guaranteed everyone complete health coverage funded by the government – socialized medicine. As always, these 42% of easily brainwashed citizens had rather have a corporate CEO, concerned about the bottom line, make decisions on their health care than a government bureaucrat.

These health care CEO's were one of the chief beneficiaries of George Bush's policies of letting all good things flow to those at the top, while ignoring the needs of the common person. As the economy grew in the early 2000's, the middle class and poor continued to lose ground and had to borrow money to keep afloat. In 2006, Americans had a savings rate of minus one percent. So, where did the economic gains go? To the top of course, where in 2008, the richest 1% received a whopping 63.5% of all income, up from 37.8% in 1980.

Americans are propagandized into believing that they can all share in the supposed great largesse that comes with free enterprise. Unfortunately, there is no such thing as free enterprise in America. Free enterprise would preclude two or three corporations from controlling 90% of most markets, as is the case in the USA. In America, corporations are so powerful that the small guy is effectively barred from market entry.

It is the great dream of Americans to own their own businesses. In truth, small businesses cannot compete in a marketplace that is controlled by the giant corporations. Depending on the source of the statistics, it is estimated that from 60% to 70% of small businesses fail within the first year, and that up to 80% fail within five years. Unfortunately, even those that are successful, wind up having to sell out to the corporate giants as they find they cannot compete in the marketplace.

Most corporations that own malls take advantage of people who have this dream of business ownership. My wife and I roam many malls, and we are always amazed at the many small shops that are in shopping centres. Then, a few years later we notice that these stores are gone, and have been replaced by another sucker's establishment who has fallen for the same free-enterprise propaganda. Getting people hooked into five and seven-year leases is how the corporate mall operators make their money. The typical mall has 50% of its spaces rented to small businesses. They know these businesses will fail within 12 to 18 months, but they have the small owner who has mortgaged his house and everything else he owns trapped into a lease that assures that the only entity making money is the corporation that owns the mall. 80% of these people fail within 5 years. Meanwhile, the big corporate stores get favourable lease terms, because of their high volume of business and large space rental.

America's economy is dominated by businesses that employ large numbers of people. Statistics indicate that the majority of American businesses employ fewer than 500 employees. Only .3% of America's businesses employ over 500 people; however, that .3% accounts for more than half of all employees and nearly 60% of the total revenue. General Motors, thanks to the Obama bail-out that saved the company and about 1.3 million total jobs, had revenues of 156 billion dollars in 2011 and a profit of 7.6 billion dollars. However, that was topped by the Wal-Mart Corporation, which had revenues of nearly 421 billion dollars in 2011 and a profit of 15.4 billion dollars. In 2011, Wal-Mart had revenues that exceeded those of 174 countries.

The egregious conduct of corporations like Wal-Mart, which closed up a store in Quebec when the workers had the courage to unionize, makes a mockery out of fair treatment of employees, and even worse, their customers. While the Walton family lives in lavish splendour, and most of them have no idea what a real day's work is like, the American employees (Canadian employees are treated better) are expected to mercilessly toil for low wages and minimum benefits. This giant behemoth of predatory capitalism can make billions extra a year by just raising the price a couple of pennies on a few items. Or, as I recently found out, by showing one price and then charging another at the register. My wife has a penchant for M & M's, but rarely buys them, because she is constantly watching her weight in case she decides to go shopping for a younger, more virile husband. So, on occasion, being the big spender that I am, I will buy her a small bag as a reward for putting up with me all these years. On a recent visit to Wal-Mart, I noticed a small bag of M & M's were only 68 cents, rather than the usual $1.08. Hey, "Diamond Wayne" decided to splurge big-time, so I threw a bag onto the checkout counter. I always watch the screen above the register to see that I am being charged the right price. For some reason, I was distracted and did not see the cashier ring-up the M & M's. As I started to leave the store, I, as usual, was checking my receipt to make sure the total was correct, and I noticed that I was charged $1.08 for the M & M's.

Livid that I was handing the Walton family an extra 40 cents, I went back to the cashier and told her in a polite way that I saw no need to give the Walton's the extra 40 cents. This minimum wage employee was very protective of her rich benefactor who expected her to toil daily for peanuts, while he enjoyed the fruits of her labour. She said that the price was always $1.08. I informed her to look at the tag on the impulse counter by the register where it clearly stated 68 cents. As a line of people waiting to spend hundreds of dollars formed at her register, she was concerned that the Walton's might be gypped out of 40 cents. Finally, exhausted trying to explain to her that she was protecting those who exploited her, I demanded to see the manager. She promptly got on the PA system and asked for a manager.

As I stood there for about five minutes waiting for a manager, I started asking myself how much my time was worth. When I used to do a lot of marketing consulting many years ago, I usually charged $175 an hour. So, I decided to start adding up my time. I waited and waited. Finally, I asked the cashier to please call the manager again. Looking at me like I was a candidate for the funny farm for being so concerned about 40 cents, she again dutifully asked for a manager.

FIGHTING FOR JUSTICE

Since I am too cheap to buy a $3.00 watch, I asked my wife to use hers to keep me apprised of the time I was spending on the vendetta against the Walton's.

Finally, two managers showed up. I suppose a deal worth 40 cents required more intelligence than could be mustered from just one brain. As this was happening, I kept a running total in my head of what it was costing the corporation to argue with me about a mere 40 cents. I was actually beginning to enjoy myself, as I get a great deal of pleasure watching those who are too dumb to realize they are slaves valiantly defending their masters who keep them in chains.

Explaining to the two burly men what had occurred, I had to walk with them to the counter and point out the sign that read, "68 cents." Somewhat taken aback that I would cause so much trouble over 40 cents, one of the managers pointed to the customer service counter and said, just go over there and get a refund.

Looking at the long line of people standing there, as two clerks tried to serve them as fast as possible, I asked myself why Wal-Mart expected their customers to stand in line, because they were too cheap to hire another minimum wage worker to keep their customers from being inconvenienced.

By then, I had decided that it was time for Wayne Frye to once again tackle the high and mighty of the corporate world. I looked at the two managers and said, "you make a mistake, and you expect me to be inconvenienced by standing in a long line to get 40 cents, because the Walton's won't hire enough clerks.

FIGHTING FOR JUSTICE

A large number of people were beginning to watch what was going on. In fact, some people who were headed out of the store stopped, stood and observed. As a trained marketer, I would have handed an irate customer the money and given him the M & M's to keep customers from seeing that I had taken advantage of someone. Not these defenders of corporate malfeasance.

One manager replied, "sir, that is our procedure for refunds."

My reply, "is it also your procedure to show one price and then leave the old price in the computer, so you can rip off your customers?"

Now, feeling like an actor delivering an academy award performance as people looked on, I continued. "You gypped me out of 40 cents. Wal-Mart has 9000 stores. If you gypped one person a store out of 40 cents each day, that means you make an extra $3600 a day for the Walton's to enjoy while your employees are lucky of they make that in a month. Multiply that by 365 days a year and you are handing those leeches an extra million dollars a year. Of course, that is peanuts to billionaires, but my guess is that you will probably gyp hundreds of customers a day with your nefarious capitalistic manipulations of unsuspecting customers who don't watch the registers the way I do. So, by the end of the year, that one 40 cent overcharge has handed the Walton's an extra 100 million dollars. Those barons of greed are not about to get an extra dime out of me. So, I want my money back and I don't intend to stand in line to get it."

FIGHTING FOR JUSTICE

By then, there were probably 25 or 30 people standing around us and perhaps that many in the McDonalds across from us, watching the sparing. The people began to applaud and one of the managers reached into his pocket and handed me $1.08.

He assumed that was the end of it, as the people continued to applaud. However, I looked at my wife and said, "how much time have I wasted on this."

She replied, "22 minutes."

I looked directly at them and said, "I don't make what the Walton's make an hour, but I get $175 an hour when I do consulting work; consequently, I am billing the Walton's for 20 minutes of my time. I am going to be generous and just send them a bill for $50."

I turned and headed out the door, as another round of applause was initiated, with my $1.08 and a free bag of M & M's. I had worked hard for them, but I gave them to my wife with a smile and said, "Wayne Frye brings another corporation to its knees. I am sure the Walton's will be shaking with fear tonight."

Obviously, the Walton's fear no one, because they are too powerful and wealthy, but I refuse to bow before greed. However, I know that I am a voice crying in the wilderness of despair, as most people just roll over and take the abuse from the wealthy and powerful and merely accept it as their lot in life. I once took my granddaughter to the grocery store, and as we were standing in a long line with just a few items in our hands , she looked over at the self-check out and said, "why don't we use the self check-out granddad?"

My reply, "because that denies someone a job, so the corporation can make more money."

She looked up at me and said, "I never thought of it that way, granddad."

Unfortunately, few people do think of it that way. That clerk's job means very little to the person who is in a hurry to get home and watch the next inane episode of *American Idol* or *Dancing with the Stars*. In a society based on greed, no one is supposed to care about the welfare of others.

Watching millions of people line up to see those royal leeches, William and Kate, as they strutted about like peacocks all over the world, makes one realize that the vast masses who are trapped in lives of quiet desperation seem to welcome their own enslavement as they worship at the altar of the privileged.

Workers have little hope of improving their lives in a system where they have no say in government policies that are skewed in favour of the corporate elite or the chosen few like the aforementioned royals. Yet, the children of these workers, who are ignored by their own government, go to schools where they are taught to admire and respect a country that has never lived up to its creed that all men are created equal. I can remember when I was a child being told by my teachers that anyone can be President. I must admit that for years, unlike most of my contemporaries, I did not believe that, but when George Bush became President, I decided that they were right, even a village idiot can become President, but only if he is from an aristocratic family with wealth and power. America's public schools serve as propaganda machines that condition young, underprivileged children to serve the needs of the all-powerful corporation by submitting to the authority of the elite. When it comes time to defend this system of inequity, it is not the sons and daughters of the elite who are expected to bear arms, but rather, the sons and daughters of the underprivileged who must die, so the children of the elite can be spared to assume their rightful place among the ruling class.

Since 1980, all the gains of the post war years for working people have been steadily eroded as membership in unions diminished due to government policies and worker complacency. All the weight of the American government now lies firmly in favour of the corporations. Even when corporations are punished for violations of worker rights, the punishments are meaningless. For example, when Wal-Mart was found to have hired sub-contractors that employed undocumented workers, they were fined a whopping $10,000, which is like fining someone like me a nickel when five of Wal Mart's owners rank among the world's top ten wealthiest people.

Most working people think that they are not smart enough to run society, because they equate intelligence with money. In reality, the smart people are not running society. Being a billionaire does not mean an individual is smart. In fact, the ruling class is nothing more than parasites feeding off the labour of those they exploit. In most cases, this wealth is passed from one generation to another. The wealthy spend most of their time in pursuit of pleasure while the working class slaves to provide them with their dividend checks. How long do you think the Bushes, Trumps, Rockefellers, Romney's or Walton's would last working the typical eight-hour day in a factory?

My father was in several businesses during his lifetime. At a very young age, he was a bootlegger, hauling the world famous North Carolina white lightning to various places throughout the south. He owned saw mills, service stations, taxicab companies, used car dealerships, mobile home dealerships, an old time lottery punch card business, a sewing machine company, several restaurants and built homes. He liked to boast that he had only lost money in one business. Although not a rich man, at one time he was very comfortable. However, my mother's seven year illness took about half his accumulated assets, because he lived in a country that is so heartless that it punishes people who have the misfortune to get sick in a nation where the basic human right of health care has been turned over to the corporate barons of greed, who suck the very life out of everything they touch. Although a business owner, he never stopped being a working man. He was not afraid to get his hands dirty to help his employees do the job that made him and them money. He hired many people down on their luck, and helped them achieve a measure of success by giving them a hand-up, when others had turned their backs.

I was also in several businesses, and I always remembered what my father once told me about being successful in business. "Wayne, you know you are successful when you help other people feed their families. I go to bed at night, feeling good, because I know that I am helping other people put food on the table by paying them a fair wage for a fair day's work."

I watched many of my Dad's employees start their own businesses over the years, and in some cases, they became more successful than my father was. However, he was always willing to help them, and in many cases, even lent them the money to get started. Like my father, I have been involved in many entrepreneurial endeavours during my life, and I never borrowed any money from him, because I always felt I had to prove that I could make it on my own just as he had. At the end of his life, as he lay dying in the hospital, unable to communicate, I bent over, kissed him on the cheek and said, "I have always been proud of you, because in spite of being a capitalist, you always treated your employees with respect and shared your bounty with them." What better epitaph for a man than to have carved on his headstone, "Here lies a capitalist who knew the meaning of compassion." If only, there were more like him.

CHAPTER 10
MY JESUS WOULDN'T

During the Vietnam War, as most service men did, I attended church regularly. It is surprising how religious one gets when faced with the prospect of being sent into battle. I was fortunate that most of my time in the service was spent in the safe environs of the Pentagon in Washington, DC. The many Christians who refused to take a stand against this immoral and illegal war, just as the vast majority of so-called Christians ignored the atrocities committed by the Unites States in its attempt to bring "democracy" to Iraq, always appalled me. Where are these worshippers of the beloved Prince of Peace when their own wonderful nation disregards everything Jesus is supposed to stand for?

These Christians turn their backs on war crimes committed by Americans, because they refuse to believe that they live in country that could commit such horrendous acts. According to official government statements, the U.S.A. does not engage in torture, rather its representatives simply practice "repetitive administration of legitimate force." Regardless of the semantics used, torture under any other name is still torture. The prisoners of war are not prisoners of war when they fight America, they are enemy combatants. In Germany, during World War II, there were no concentration camps; they were detention centres, according to the Germans. The Christians would vilify any government that operated a concentration camp, even if it went by a more innocuous name. Why were they not up in arms over

America operating "detention centres" at Guantanamo Bay and Abu Ghraib? Obama vowed that he would close up Guantanamo Bay, but, as usual, he wilted under Republican pressure. Today, that blot on human decency still operates, and the Jesus lovers continue to sit idly by with no protestations whatsoever.

Being an Arab or Muslim is an invitation for torture by the U.S. government. Apparently, Christians have no concern for people like 22-year old taxi driver Ahmed Dilawar, who was reportedly chained by his wrists to the top of his cell for four days and had his legs beaten (called "personal strikes" by the government) to the point that he could no longer stand. According to a witness, his tormentors laughed at him and lined up to strike him while shouting, "Allah." He was found hanged in his cell, which contained no chair for him to stand on. However, it was deemed a suicide. Meanwhile, Christians and churches ignored this and other examples of torture. How many Dilawars must there be, before these so-called compassionate Christians band together and demand a government that respects their beloved saviour's ideals?

Bigotry and intolerance seem to be considered a virtue by most fundamentalist Christians. How else can you explain the prominence of the televangelists who spew out hatred on Sundays through vast media outlets that feed the unquestioning masses a steady stream of judgmental propaganda? While these paragons of virtue ride around in Rolls Royce's, dine in the best restaurants, wear $3000 tailor-made suits and live in opulent palaces of splendour, they never attack the American greed that denies citizens health care, decent places to live, jobs that pay reasonable wages or speak out for a sensible system of taxation where the rich pay their fair share. They are too busy attacking immorality, abortion and the gay lifestyle to be concerned with the mundane things like poverty or injustice.

General George Pace, former U.S. Army Chief of Staff, in 2006 said, "I believe a homosexual act between two individuals is immoral and that we should never condone immoral acts." Here is an individual who trains men and women to maim and kill in the name of democracy, invades a country without any provocation, allows prisoners of war to be tortured, approves the killing of innocent civilians, and he has the nerve to say two people of the same sex who engage in a sexual relationship are immoral. This kind of moral hypocrisy makes religion in America nothing more than an exercise in judgemental arrogance.

The issue of global warming is ignored by the mainstream churches in America, but if someone could prove that gay sex was the cause of global warming, the pulpits of America would be filled with ministers urging the government to stop global warming by making homosexual acts illegal. Americans are in a religious bubble that insulates them from a real understanding of the serious issues facing the world. If they would spend less time in church and less time praying, they might actually be able to tackle some of the serious problems that are plaguing humanity. If God is such a benevolent being, would he rather Christians spend Sundays in church, or spend the day passing out food to the poor, or opening their so-called

Christian homes to those with no roof over their heads. Why don't the churches, which sit unused most of the time, open up their doors and allow the homeless to come in out of the cold and sleep on a nice warm pew for the evening? Rather than building a fancy edifice to the glory of God, why don't these good Christians build a homeless shelter or offer free childcare for the working people of America who cannot afford the luxury of leaving their children in day-care.

One should never underestimate the power of religiously inspired hate. Throughout history, the church has been at the forefront in the suppression of dissent while ignoring the plight of the poor who are relegated to the fringes of a society based on greed. Today, these ministers of mayhem often equate Christianity with capitalism. No system of government based on greed could ever be part of the Jesus I learned about in Sunday school. The various religious denominations are nothing more than corporate entities, desperately trying to increase their profits by selling more of their product. Just like Wal-Mart and General Motors, they must be constantly looking for new customers to maintain or broaden their market share. Jesus is like every other commodity in America, he must be effectively marketed to the customers.

History has shown that religion is not the answer to poverty; rather, it is, in most cases, the precursor to poverty. When people see no way out, they do not attack the powerful. Rather, they turn to religion and take solace in the minister who assures them that they will receive their reward in the end. In most communities, these ministers are not only part of the powerful class, but also part of the well-off, if not wealthy class.

Being from the south, I was always amazed at the tales of the Civil War, or as the southerners called it, *The War for Southern Independence*, because while the rich slaveholders bought their way out of military service, the poor whites fought the federal troops so the rich could keep their plantations and slaves. There were many cases where even the slaves joined up to fight against their own freedom, because they felt bound to serve their masters.

In the United States, the poor are constantly encouraged to fight enemies that do not really exist. The government identifies enemies like Iraq, which had absolutely nothing to do with 9/11, while the religious leaders take aim at a permissive, immoral society that is an offence to God. Rather than wailing against homosexuality and abortion to their poor church members, fundamentalist ministers should be attacking appalling poverty in the richest country in the world.

In today's homophobic America, religious leaders attack the gay lifestyle as an abomination in the eyes of God. Gay people, therefore, are denied the right to marry in most states or have equal access to health care and jobs, because they are evil. I will not take the time to go back in history to cite times when the church did sanctify same sex marriages, but let it suffice to say that the church is even more bigoted and exclusionary today than it was before 1400, when same sex unions were permitted by many religious organizations.

FIGHTING FOR JUSTICE

No political leader in America can be elected by overtly supporting gay rights. Even Bill Clinton knew that when he signed the Defence of Marriage Act in order to pander to the religious right wing. In addition, his attempt to make it possible to allow gays to serve openly in the U.S. Military, like they are allowed to do in all the western European armies, Israel and the Canadian military, led to the infamous "don't ask, don't tell policy," which actually resulted in more people being discharged from the military for homosexuality than ever before. Fortunately, this is one of the few things that Obama actually stood up to the Republicans on, as he finally dispatched this arcane approach to the dust bin of history and now gays are allowed to serve openly in the U.S. military like most other civilized countries. Although, one can be assured that once back in the White House, the Republicans, will, no doubt, make an effort to repeal this law that they consider an affront to God. Perhaps, at the same time, they will pass laws that will allow a return to the times when men could sell their daughters to the highest bidder or kill a rebellious son. Don't you just love the Old Testament?

Clinton learned a valuable lesson from President Lyndon Johnson, who, upon signing the Civil Rights Act of 1964, said that with one stroke of the pen he was doing the right thing, but doing the right thing would make the south turn against the Democratic Party for generations. This dire prediction came true as the south had trouble putting its racist past behind it, and is firmly in the hands of the Republican Party today. How many white ministers stood up in their pulpits and told their congregations that Jesus was an equal opportunity saviour? I can remember ministers saying that the Civil Rights Act was the beginning of the end for Christianity as God, himself, had separated the races, according to the Bible. So, whether homosexuality or the mixing of races, the church has a sordid history of doing the wrong thing.

Where do the paragons of virtue who stand in the pulpits of America get their religious doctrines? The Hebrew Old Testament clearly states that King David had a sexual relationship with Jonathan, the son of King Saul. Ironically, King James, who ordered the translation of the Bible that is the most widely used today, was himself, a homosexual. It is well known that the translators were homophobic, and secretly changed passages as a way to get back at a King they considered despicable, and whom they knew would not take the time to read their entire translation.

When I used to have a television, I often watched televangelists, because I find their ranting, raving manipulation and pontificating as entertaining as any program on television. When I taught marketing in university, I always encouraged my students to watch televangelists as the perfect example of how to effectively market a product.

It is particularly interesting to see how vehement ministers are in support of Israel. Yet, these religious paragons of virtue, just as does the U.S. government, forget that it was the Israelis who were called terrorists by many western countries when they were trying to form the state of Israel. Almost ever Israeli Prime Minister since 1948 has been a former member of the army or a clandestine guerrilla group. The beloved and revered Prime Minister Menachem Begin was head of the feared Irgun Zvai Leumi movement, and has long been rumoured to have been involved in one of the most horrific terrorist acts of all time, the bombing of the King David Hotel.

The Bible is filled with acts of terrorism by the followers of God. One of the best examples is the terrorist act performed by Samson to get back at his tormentors. The temple was crowded with men, women and children. Yes, they were all Philistines, but were even the little children supposed to pay for mocking Samson. What kind of God would slaughter the innocent to get at the guilty? Supposedly, there were in excess of 3,000 people watching Samson as he called out to Yahweh, "Lord remember me. Give me strength this last time, and let me be avenged at one blow for my two eyes." With his arms around the two central pillars supporting the building, his right arm around one and his left arm around the other, he cried out, "let me die with the Philistines." He leaned forward with all his strength and the temple fell on the chiefs and on all the people who were in it. He killed more people at his death than he had killed in his entire life." (Judges 16: 27-30)

The Bible is full of acts of violence, all done in the name of God. Is that why America thinks it is justified in using violence throughout the world to suppress others to its Christian inspired will?

Why do religious leaders vilify Hamas and Hezbollah, while saying nothing about Israeli violations of human rights in the occupied territories? The height of hypocrisy was George Bush, with the support of religious leaders, calling for free elections in Gaza and the West Bank, but when these free elections put in a Hamas administration, America immediately withdrew all political and financial support. In other words, have free elections as long as you elect someone who can be controlled by America. Why did the religious leaders not speak out against this hypocrisy by their beloved Bible-thumping President?

Unfortunately, most Americans do not realize that the churches they attend are nothing more than subsidiaries of vast denominational corporations whose goal is to increase revenue just like all corporations. This is truer today than ever before, as religious denominations build their corporate empires that offer the elite officers in the company exorbitant salaries and benefits. For example, for years the Vatican offered subsidized housing to help the poor in Rome, but in 2007, they decided their benevolence was costing them too much revenue; consequently, they demanded the residents move or pay much higher rents as the Vatican wanted to convert the residences to hotels or commercial enterprises that would generate more revenue. Many residents had their rents tripled from $1000 a month to $3000 a month. Ironically, some of these apartment buildings were actually donated to the church for use in serving the poor people. Many of these residents lived in the buildings since World War II, but were told to vacate in order for the capitalistic church to practice the very thing it often preaches against, greed. One of the buildings was converted into the St. George Hotel, which now serves the elite of the world in $600 a night rooms. It is much more important for the church to provide the wealthy with a well-appointed room so they can enjoy the fruits of their success, than to provide the starving poor with a roof over their heads for a reasonable fee. The church has definitely decided to get its priorities in order by making capitalism an integral part of Christianity.

In the United States, the churches are involved in a variety of capitalistic endeavours from running amusement parks to operating large mail order businesses that ship the believers a variety of merchandise that will make them more likely to get into heaven. Meanwhile, the multi-million dollar church owned property is tax exempt.

While America's churches go on their merry way, listening to the soft flutter of 20 dollar bills floating gently into the collection plates, they never call the American government to task for ignoring the one thing that Jesus would be most concerned about, social justice. While George Bush was obliterating Baghdad with weapons of mass destruction, killing innocent men, women and children, the churches were all busy justifying revenge for the 9/11 attacks. Even though Iraq had nothing to do with 9/11, the invasion of Iraq was justified, because it was an evil country anyway, since it was filled with despicable heathens who had the audacity to worship Mohammad as the messenger of God, rather than Jesus.

Revenge is at the very heart of the American Christian creed, as seldom do you hear any of the American Christian leaders urging the U.S.

government to turn the other cheek as Jesus did. Jesus also said: "You have been taught an eye for an eye and a tooth for a tooth, but I say do not resist evil. If someone hits you, let them hit you twice. If someone sues you in court to get your coat, give it to him and your cloak, too. If someone asks you for something, give it to him. If he wants to borrow money, give it freely. Give all you have to the poor."

How many ministers standing in the American fundamentalist pulpits on Sundays do you hear using these quotes from Jesus? These skilled manipulators have completely perverted the message of Jesus. Showing love and forgiveness is seen as a sign of weakness in a society that uses its military and economic might to impose its will on country after country. Punishing the "evil doers," as George "I Love Jesus" Bush liked to call anyone who opposed America, is the new moral imperative. Rather than the peace-loving Jesus of the New Testament, American Christians have reverted to the vengeful, wrathful God of the Old Testament.

The modern day Fundamentalists look to the Republicans as the party of Jesus. Yet, this is the same party that refuses to provide universal health care, abhors a raise in the minimum wage because it might cut into business profits and ignores the great disparity between the haves and have-nots. Further, it promulgates a tax structure that allows the wealthy to escape fair and equitable taxation, and spends obscene amounts of money on weapons to kill and maim the citizens of other nations, while allowing its own citizens to be subjected to the most adverse poverty in the First World. Meanwhile, its political leaders ballyhoo the merits of this bankrupt idea of corporate exploitation, as if it is part of the Judeo-Christian tradition.

Does any real caring Christian think Jesus would be a capitalist, urging people to look out only for themselves and to pile up all the riches they can, regardless of the effect it might have on fellow citizens? Or, would Jesus be a socialist, who encourages the populace to look after one another and provide for the common welfare in a fair economic system?

Fundamentalist Christians look to politicians in the Republican Party as representatives of their beloved Christ. George Bush was the Fundamentalists' dream leader who was supposed to make the government more Godly. Unfortunately, these Christians were too delusional to see that Bush was more representative of the anti-Christ than of Jesus, as he turned the government over to a pack of fascist, corporate-loving, bottom-feeding thieves who bankrupted the country and savaged the futures of countless generations who will be saddled with the bills run up by these warmongering, elitist denizens of right-wing ideology.

If these Jesus-loving fundamentalists wanted to find the 20th century's most Christ-like idealist, they should have revered the man who turned his back on a life of affluence as a physician in Argentina. This man said, "I could have had a comfortable life as a physician and helped many people, but I decided I could help more people by being a revolutionary than by being a physician." This man was Ernesto "Che" Guevara, who saw revolution as the only effective way to fight poverty in a world awash in vast riches that are concentrated in far too few hands. Unlike the George Bush's and the Mitt Romney's of the world, he did not view his affluence and family connections as a panacea that would make his life easy. Although an atheist, I believe that "Che" would have said, "if this Jesus did exist, the man I read about in the Bible was not crucified because he was meek and mild, he was crucified because he was a revolutionary who tried to transform a corrupt, uncaring society. His struggle still goes on today. All those who truly love Jesus love the idea of revolution against the oppressors."

I am amazed at how Christians rant and rave about the Godlessness of modern man, but the truth is that the belligerence of America can be traced to economics and religion. The people who brought down the World Trade Centre believed they were doing God's work, just as Americans thought they were doing God's work when they rained down bombs from the sky to destroy Baghdad.

It took centuries to curb the excesses practiced by a variety of religions in America, but with the appointment of George Bush as President in 2000, the doors of religious repression were swung wide open again and a complete assault on secularism was untaken by a government intent on making sure that "freedom of religion" did not mean "freedom from religion." In America, even the Democratic candidates (Obama included) are now making appearances, professing the important role faith plays in their lives.

FIGHTING FOR JUSTICE

Religion has never set the standard for morality. In fact, religion has been at the forefront of many repressive societies that are anything but moral. Fear and intimidation are integral parts of religious doctrine. Fear of the devil, fear of hell and fear of God's wrath are used to keep the people in line. When the church insisted the world was flat, scientists were termed heretics for suggesting the world was round. These same scientists were excommunicated when they had the audacity to suggest the earth revolved around the sun, rather than the sun revolving around the earth. Questioning the authority of the church has always led to serious repercussions, whether done in 1207 or 2012. The church is infallible – according to the church.

In my opinion, it makes no difference whether you reach God through Lord Krishna, Confucius, Buddha, Mohammad, Jesus or a head of cabbage. If there is a God, I do not think he or she is egomaniacal enough to askew good works and only base admittance to eternity on belief in the messenger, rather than belief in compassion, which should be the basis for all who seek grace. If he is the type of God who would send a young child who dies at a young age without accepting Christ to hell, he is not the kind of God I would want to spend eternity with anyway. The idea that only those of a certain religion will be in heaven is part of the problem with American Christianity. The arrogance of self-righteousness is not very Jesus-like at all.

Too many religious leaders have turned Jesus into a personal moneymaking machine. Playing the age-old bait and switch game, they offer a cure for all men's ills with a healthy dose of Jesus Christ. Fundamentalist Christians have great reverence for Jim Bakker, Benny Hinn, Pat Robertson, Jerry Falwell, Paul Crouch, Robert Schuller, Billy Graham, Franklin Graham and other orators of the faith who stand behind their gold-plated rostrums or sit on their $50,000 dollar sofas with $250,000 Steinway pianos in the background. The poor boobs who fall for their spellbinding promises of a primrose path to heaven dutifully send in their money so these pontificators of profundity can live in their splendorous mansions, fly in their private jets and air condition their doghouses.

There is an old saying that you should never speak ill of the dead, but when the dead have been finger pointing, hypocritical, deceptive, sanctimonious Pharisees I think they are fair game. While researching the first edition of this book in 2007, Jerry Falwell died. I was amazed at the constant coverage of his death on American television. If they were going to cover him at all, what they should have covered was not his influence on the American political scene, but his incredible record of bigotry, intolerance and war mongering. His stands against women's rights and his bigoted ravings against homosexuality are legendary. Who can forget his attack on teletubbies, because he defined them as "gay?" Of course, his constant attacks on Godless public education and the ACLU were also extremely voracious and savage.

Early in his ministry, Falwell was an avowed segregationist, vehemently attacking the civil rights movement and its leader, Dr. Martin Luther King. He even insisted that it was God, himself, who instituted the black tribe of Ham represented by Noah's bad son. God ordained separation through his acts in the Old Testament.

Therefore, it was only natural that Falwell was an avid supporter of the apartheid regime in South Africa as well as the many violent dictatorships in Latin America. Fascist regimes were considered defenders of God's will.

Falwell declared that AIDS was simply the result of rampant sins among homosexuals who were now paying the price for turning their backs on God's admonition not to engage in same-sex relationships. It was also about this time that he made the famous statement that feminists were just women who needed a man to tell them what to do.

When Bush launched his illegal, immoral war of conquest on Iraq, Falwell declared, "we need to take the battle to heathen Muslims, and do unto them before they do unto us." Of course, this could be expected from a man who said the 9/11 attacks were God's punishment for America's toleration of abortion, feminism, homosexuality and liberalism. If people like Falwell are ordained by God, it certainly makes one question God's judgment.

Republican politicians were quick to heap praise on Falwell. Even Mitt Romney, who as a Mormon was, no doubt, considered a heathen by Falwell, made a great effort to talk about his positive influence on the spiritual lives of so many Americans. Many other Republican politicians made it a point to show up at his funeral, so they could be photographed showing homage to this monument of right wing, religious hypocrisy.

Falwell's ministry was a supporter of corporate exploitation, as he received a great deal of donations from corporations, who saw fundamentalist religion as an excellent vehicle to control the working class who were predominantly fundamentalists. This led to the fundamentalist ministers overwhelmingly equating Christianity with capitalism.

Falwell's founding of the Moral Majority was neither a moral endeavour nor a majority. It was simply a group of influential so-called Christians who decided that they could con their followers into believing that putting Jesus loving Republicans in office would make things better. In reality, their real goal was to exert an inordinate amount of control over public officials so they could shove their so-called morals and perverted ideas of what Jesus stands for down all Americans throats.

The death of Falwell in no way slowed inroads made by those who want to turn America into a theocracy just as the Taliban did in Afghanistan. The place of God is assured in American government forever, as even the Democrats have learned that the road to political power is lined with flag-waving, Jesus loving despots who cannot countenance any idea of a secular government. Religion is as American as apple pie, and for that reason, the American government will always dance to the tune of the intolerant, bigoted, finger-pointing, corporate-loving, perverted bastions of morality who call themselves Christians, but who are in reality an affront to everything that Jesus stood for.

It is very interesting how morality must always be defined by those who interpret the Bible for those of us who are somehow too dumb to read and think for ourselves. I often wonder how many people have really read the Bible and given it serious thought, rather than letting "interpreters" do the thinking for them. As a child, I could not get my hands on very many sex books or magazines, and of course, the internet was unavailable; consequently, one of my favourite sex books was the Bible. Yes, you read right, the Bible. I wonder how many times I read *The Song of Solomon*. Now any boy approaching puberty can certainly find its vivid sexual descriptions almost as exciting as reading a few paragraphs from *Playboy*.

That is the reason why I find the story of another unsung hero, Linette Servais, so interesting. As a church organist, she was unparalleled in her musical ability, but sexual suppression by her church showed that free thought and religion are not compatible. Linette was unceremoniously removed after serving 35 years as choir director and organist, because the priest decided that her sale of sex toys was not consistent with church teachings. Which immediately makes one reflect on the fact that the church often did not remove priests from their duties when it was found that they were engaged in pedophilia?

Servais went to work for Pure Romance Company due to mounting hospital bills not covered by the

Jesus-loving government of George Bush at the time, as a brain tumour had not only had an obvious financial effect on her, but also left her sexually dysfunctional. She took the job for financial reasons, but also because it afforded her an opportunity to lend assistance to other women who were having similar problems.

When her priest told her that she had to make a decision between playing the organ and representing Pure Romance, Servais prayed over the matter and to her credit decided that her ministry to help women deal with sexual dysfunction was more important than leading the choir or playing the organ. Linette Servais should serve as an example to all Christians who need to exercise more intestinal fortitude in standing up to religious intolerance and bigotry, rather than following the pronouncements of a few self-appointed, sanctimonious interpreters of God's word.

The cruelty of God in the Bible is as violent as any R-rated movie ever produced. Here are just a few of the hundreds of examples: Men are urged to keep the young virgins for pleasure, all the first born in Egypt are killed even though they are too young to even know about God, captured people are slaughtered – 12,000 in one instance alone, polygamy is sanctioned and daughters are sold to the highest bidder.

I wonder how many Christians seriously consider what Revelations says about only 144,000 believers going to heaven and everyone else going to hell. And what about the admonition to avoid eating swine, does that mean every Christian who has sampled bacon or ham is doomed to hell? What about the verse that says, "dogs, sorcerers, whoremongers, idolaters, and anyone who ever told a lie will not enter the Kingdom of Heaven." How many Christians have never told a lie, even to their parents when they were children? They conveniently ignore the musings that might make them squeamish about their own chances for heaven, but they are quick to ridicule anyone who does not believe that a man lived in the belly of a whale or that a man was able to get two of every animal in the world on a boat the size of a couple of football fields. And how do they explain God making two people who eventually populated the entire world without any incest being committed. A complete suspension of reason is a requirement for anyone who genuinely believes everything written in holy books, and America is filled with people who have completely turned their thinking over to a pack of sanctimonious, finger-pointing Pharisees. It is always easier to let others do your thinking for you.

Does any reasonable thinking individual with an modicum of compassion think that Jesus would sanction an economic system that enslaves the poor and middle class to serve the rich? The American economy blatantly rewards greed. In fact, greed is considered good in America, as it is the pursuit of wealth that forms the basis of what America is all about. Getting rich is the noblest ambition, as Ronald Reagan said, "let the rich get richer, because the benefits tickle down to the rest of us, because a rising tide raises all boats." That was easy for people like Reagan to say, because he was part of the rising tide, but the truth is that most people get pulled under the waves of a rising tide and sink to the bottom while the yachts sail into the horizon.

The government is not supposed to help people in America, because it makes them dependent on a hand out. Yet, the very people who vehemently attack this socialistic approach have no problem accepting government contracts when they are in business. Does Dick Cheney really think he would be a multi-millionaire if it were not for his government contacts that led Halliburton to hire him after Bush I? George Bush had the taxpayers bail him out when the Texas Rangers were foundering. Yet, these two men of God, refused to reach out with the hand of compassion to others who would like a little of the government largesse that made these two bastions of morality immensely wealthy. Only the wealthy are allowed to gorge at the public trough, while the poor are told to pick up the scraps. The real welfare in America is distributed to the wealthy, not the poor.

Jesus spoke often about poverty and its effect on humanity. Was it not he who said, "do not lay up treasures on earth. Go, sell what you have and give it to the poor." It was also he who said as the rich turned their backs on his message, "it is easier for a camel to go through the eye of a needle than for a rich man to enter the kingdom of God.

It is Jesus who said, "forgive your debtors and give to everyone who begs from you." So, does this sound like a man who thinks a hand out is wrong? Jesus saw moral decay in those who refused to share their wealth, not in those who accepted a hand out.

FIGHTING FOR JUSTICE

America is capable of feeding the entire world's population, but it does not do so, because of economics. Flooding the market with food would drive down the price and affect the bottom line of too many corporations. Consequently, billions of people go to bed hungry every night, not because of a food shortages, but because of economic principles that dictate a policy of benign neglect of the needs of the poor. Ironically, people like George Bush, who talked about their Christian compassion, forget the Bible states very clearly that it is the responsibility of the rulers to create a just society. Of course, to these arrogant scions of privilege, a just society is one where all wealth flows to the top, and the poor suckers at the bottom are just oil to grease the wheels of economic servitude.

Religion, economics and politics in America have merged, but the three are not representative of what Jesus stood for. Jesus was the original bleeding heart liberal, who saw injustice in a system that promulgated too great a disparity between the rich and poor. If people are truly followers of the Prince of Peace, they would not be Democrat or Republican. They would support socialism, which is a system that guarantees equality of opportunity and a fair distribution of wealth.

If America's leaders were such devoted followers of the Prince of Peace, they would abstain from voting themselves obscene salaries and benefits and give the excess money to the poor. If George Bush had been a really good Christian, he would have assigned his $200,000 a year Presidential pension to an orphanage or a children's hospital, and just drawn from his trust fund in old age. He might even assign his taxpayer paid health care benefits to some poor people who can't get the life saving operation they need.

I know Christians are not interested in my interpretation of Jesus, but for the few who might be reading this book with an open mind, simply ask yourself this question: "Would Jesus support an economic system based on greed?"

My Jesus wouldn't.

CHAPTER 11
PREACHING LOVE AND PRACTICING HATE

Thousands of Americans who died fighting Fascism and Nazism in World War II would be horrified that in little more than sixty years the American people would sit idly by and witness without protest the takeover of their government by the multi-national Nazi-like corporate cabals and the religious fascist purveyors of deceit. Paralyzed by the manipulation of the corporate controlled media and the ministers of religious subterfuge, most Americans' brains are nothing more than mush that absorbs flag-waving patriotism and capitalistic propaganda like Bounty paper towels soaking up liquid. America, like the Nazis these brave men and women helped to destroy, engaged in torture and practiced mass murder by turning its corporate-backed military machine lose to rain bombs on innocent women and children in Iraq and Afghanistan. One might think this ended with the Bush Administration, but Obama continued both wars and even revved up the drone strikes that he thinks are permissible when the military identifies a terrorist target. My question is, "how do you identify a terrorist?" To many countries, the USA is a terrorist nation. Do those countries have the right to send drones to attack targets in the USA? The convoluted thinking of Americans justifies all acts committed by their nation, because it is always in the right. For example, it is the USA that gets to decide what countries can have nuclear weapons. It is perfectly acceptable for Israel, that practices apartheid against the Palestinians, to have nuclear weapons, but Iran is not allowed to have them, because the USA says so.

FIGHTING FOR JUSTICE

Americans care more about who will be the next *American Idol* winner than how many people their nation kills in its wars of conquest, how many people are homeless or how many lose their life-savings because they have the misfortune to get sick.

Bush's lavish tax cuts for the wealthy would have funded a free college education for every American during its first five years. Just imagine all the health care, education, mortgage assistance and veterans benefits that could have been funded with the nearly one trillion dollars in tax breaks afforded the people making over $200,000 a year. And what about the other trillion dollars that went into inflecting senseless pain and suffering on the people of Iraq in an unjustified, illegal and immoral war that was based on a mountain of lies and deception?

Ironically, these lies are perpetrated by those who herald their devotion to Jesus. Bush, who proclaimed Jesus as the most profound influence in his life, was propelled into office by those who deemed him a man of God. In a nation where poor people buy plane tickets they cannot afford, to take a journey to see a grilled cheese sandwich that supposedly has an image of Jesus Christ, it is not difficult to understand why most Americans fall prey to those who declare their devotion to Jesus. Fairy tales are interwoven into the very fabric of what America is all about. In Fostoria, Ohio, the community actually put up flood lights to shine on a soybean storage tank that was attracting thousands of visitors to look at rust stains on the side of the tank that looked like an image of Christ standing behind a small boy.

Newspapers and television stations actually reported this nonsense as if it was news, without mentioning that there were never any paintings that were done of Jesus while he was alive, so no one has any idea what he actually looked like. Then again, what should one expect from news media that headlines their shows with stories about Britney Spears, Paris Hilton, Angelina Jolie, Brad Pitt and the latest antics of the Kardashians.

Of course, maybe images of Christ should be news, but not in the way the buffoons of network news report it. It should be explored as an important story, because it illustrates that most Americans are credulous non-thinkers, easily manipulated by the media, religious leaders and politicians who play them like a fine tuned Stradivarius.

It is particularly frightening to think that these same people, with their shallow, easily manipulated minds and child-like perceptions of reality are the ones who actually vote for the politicians who represent these fanatical ideas and wind up running the country. Unfortunately, Americans are too wrapped up in these fairy-tales to realize that they have everything to lose and nothing to gain by supporting a government that loves Jesus, but does nothing to promulgate the very ideals for which Jesus is supposed to stand.

So, it easy to see that many of the problems in the USA are not just rooted in an unjust economic system; they are a result of religious fervour. There is actually a malevolent nature to this deceit that is practiced as part of religion. Fundamentalist Christians often lie to themselves, thinking they know and practice "the word of God." However, in reality these people are perpetuating intolerance by not practicing what their beloved Jesus actually taught.

How many Christians preach love, but practice hatred, resentment and abhorrence by being intolerant toward specific groups of people and advocating the righteous sanctification of war, even justifying the murder and torture of men, women and children to exact revenge for acts of aggression against America. There is an innate arrogance in those who think they are righteous while they point the finger of condemnation at all who do not follow their definition of moral and immoral. Can the Fundamentalist Christians who want to turn America into a theocracy not see that makes them no different than the fundamentalist Muslims that they hold up to ridicule?

I am so thankful to be a Canadian citizen. Canadians are so much more cognizant of the need to make sure that religion is not allowed to unduly influence the decisions of government. Canada is a compassionate society that allows capitalism to flourish, without the harshness and callousness that is such a profound element of the U.S. economic structure. Yet, most Americans look with disdain on Canada and call it a socialist country, because we care enough to provide universal health care and afford the most vulnerable a social safety net that prevents the abject poverty that is so prevalent in America. Of course, there are still elements here that would like to take this country on the same path as the USA. Fortunately, Canadians are not as easy to manipulate with religion and patriotism.

FIGHTING FOR JUSTICE

I know many American Christians who vehemently proclaim the USA as a defender of all that is moral and right in the world, and everyone of them comes from the upper middle class that makes up about 12% of Americans. Sure they think America is great, because they have good-paying jobs, their employers provide health insurance, and they are guaranteed a good pension. These people are looked after by a society that takes care of the well-off, while those who toil in the grimy factories and the dusty fields have no future and no hope. Is this Christian? Would Jesus approve? How can any middle or upper middle class American Christian face Jesus and say there is nothing wrong with the way America treats the underprivileged? Was it not Jesus himself who admonished the well-off to give all they have to the poor?

These same Christians defended a pseudo-Christian in the White House who lied about weapons of mass destruction, approved the torture of prisoners as young as 15 and mercilessly killed between 150,000 to 300,000 innocent men, women and children attacking a country in retaliation for an act it did not even commit. The lies are obvious, but the fundamentalist Christians of America are so convinced of their righteousness that lies to cover up lies are accepted as truth. Meanwhile, these bastions of probity proudly parade into church every Sunday feeling no remorse for supporting these abominations committed by their leaders.

While Americans rallied to the cause after 9/11, and Bush boldly said he would "root out" the terrorists, the fundamentalist Christians pledged to bring the wrath of God down upon those who dared attack America.

However, when Hurricane Katrina hit New Orleans, these same Christians did not demand that the wrath of God be brought down on George Bush and his ineffectual government for spending money on bombs and bullets rather than building levees to protect the citizens of New Orleans. While America ignores infrastructure to build weapons, the Europeans build massive dykes and levees to protect their people. America had rather bomb foreign countries and give tax breaks to the wealthy than spend money to protect its own citizens.

The catastrophic collapse of the I-35 Bridge in Minnesota is a direct result of America having its priorities askew. The state of Minnesota found the money to build a $500,000,000 domed stadium to house the pro-sports teams of billionaires, but it could not justify spending the money to retrofit a bridge that was on the verge of falling down. This kind of convoluted thinking is at the very heart of an economic system that is supported by a pack of hypocritical Bible thumpers who seem to think that being a Christian and being a money-grubbing capitalist is the same thing.

The fundamentalist Christians are more concerned about abortion or two men having sex with each other than they are about real social issues like universal health care, a fair wage, homelessness, unjust wars or the disparity between the rich and the poor. Which issues would Jesus be most concerned with? Did Jesus every concern himself with homosexuality? One might even question the sexual orientation of 13 men who consistently lived together without women around.

FIGHTING FOR JUSTICE

Could the brilliant interpreters of the Bible be ignoring something?

Religion in America is a big supporter of the status-quo. Questioning any authority is considered non-Christian, as long as there is a Republican in the White House that is. Of course, when a heathen like Bill Clinton was President, the Christians were perfectly willing to attack authority to protect people from the devil-inspired manifestations of universal health care or allowing gays to serve openly in the military. These moral do-gooders were much more concerned about a White House blow job than the real issues that faced an America that had been paralyzed by Congressional Republicans blocking important social legislation. Then, along comes Barrack Obama, who has really gotten the right wing into an uproar. Less a socialist than 1950's Republican President Dwight Eisenhower, he is branded a communist by the right wing that just cannot accept the fact that an Africa-American is in the White House. Ironically, he is not even an African-American, as his mother was white.

Fundamentalist Christians think all problems can be solved with prayer. Maybe they are right, but what they should be praying for is to have God give the politicians and the rich some compassion for the working class, so they could share the bounty with the less fortunate.

These patrons of Jesus actually believe that putting the Ten Commandments up in school hallways will make children learn more and be better behaved. This is at the very heart of the indoctrination syndrome that is perpetrated by church leaders who know that you must get young children in Sunday school at an early age, so that the brainwashing can be done before they develop cognitive skills that might actually lead to them questioning authority. When authority is questioned, those in power become very nervous, because a population that thinks for themselves might revolt against the control of the wealthy and powerful.

I never cease to be amazed by people who turn their lives over to God, and all of a sudden, God has a plan for them. Do they ever stop to think that maybe God had a plan for them when they had not turned their lives over to him? Maybe he wanted them to be bad, so others could use them as an example of what not to be. I heard a person on a television news program many years ago say that he got the licence number of a man who kidnapped a girl and killed her. He said that it was God's will that he be there, so the man could be captured. Does he ever stop to think where God was when the girl was kidnapped and murdered? Maybe she was bad, so God decided it was time to dispatch her. Those kinds of statements attest to the absolute inability of many religious people to think logically.

When Rudy Giuliani was running for the Republican nomination for President, I always found it interesting how he kept bringing up the fact that he was a man of faith, because he knew that he had to get the votes of Fundamentalist Christians, who are the core of the Republican party. That was the only thing he mentioned as much as 9/11. In fact, someone once said that all Giuliani's sentences contained three things: a noun , a verb and 9/11. I am so sick of hearing the term

FIGHTING FOR JUSTICE

9/11. Americans act like they are the only ones to ever suffer atrocities, when, in fact, it is America, its corporate masters and its religious supporters who have perpetrated atrocity after atrocity all over the globe. The Christians love to wave the flag and proclaim the righteousness of America, but if they were really doing God's work, they would demand the dismantling of the military-industrial complex that is strangling the USA with its noose that hangs around a government that neglects the real needs of the people.

Hugo Chavez has been called a dictator by U.S. politicians and the corporate media. It is interesting that he would be called a dictator in America, when he was popularly elected in a free and open election that was monitored by no less than the Carter Centre in Atlanta. How hypocritical of a country like the USA, where a man was appointed President in 2000, even though he lost the popular vote, to brand a man who actually won the popular vote a dictator. What would that have made George Bush?

Chavez is a Catholic, as are most of the people in Venezuela, so he interestingly turned to religion when he gave a profound speech before the United Nations on September 20, 2006. A speech that was only paraphrased by the U.S. media, and very poorly interpreted from Spanish into English by biased newscasters.

Due to space constraints, I will not go into great detail, but he actually appealed to the religious people in America to recognize what their government was doing. Unfortunately, he delivered the speech in

Spanish, which meant that most Americans never heard the real speech. And as typical of Americans, they let their leaders and the media interpret the speech for them, without ever reading the English transcribed version that was readily available on the internet or from the United Nations archives. After all, reading what he actually said would take some effort and some thinking, which, unfortunately, Americans prefer to let others do for them.

In his speech, he encouraged Americans to read Noam Chomsky's, *Hegemony or Survival: The Imperialist Strategy of the United States.* (Of course, I am sure the religious right wing, the Republicans and even most Democrats never bothered to read it, as it would take some effort and even some of the aforementioned thinking for themselves as referenced in the previous paragraph.)

Chavez boldly spoke of how the American empire was placing at risk the very survival of the human species. He appealed to the good people of the United States, and particularly those of religious conviction, to halt this threat, which is like a sword hanging over people's heads. Rather than cover the positives in his speech, the media decided to highlight his references to George Bush's previous speech as arrogant and one-sided.

Insulting the President of the USA by saying the rostrum still smelled of sulphur, indicating the devil had been there, was more important than covering the reasons Chavez had said that. Meanwhile, Bush's arrogant speech attacking other countries was not even critiqued, as it is perfectly alright for American to be disrespectful of other leaders and countries. Again, the hypocrisy is almost mind-boggling.

I am very proud of a letter I received from Hugo Rafael Chavez Frias, Senor Presidente de la Republica Bolivariana de Venezuela after he got a copy of my 2006 book, *The Catastrophic Calamities of a Village Idiot in the Real Evil Empire*. The copy of a book he sent me, *Simon Bolivar*, is displayed, along with the letter, in a prominent place in my library. I just hope the next time he holds up a book, it will be a copy of mine. (I could use the publicity and increased sales generated by such an act.)

A few years ago, weary and discouraged after years of trying to effectuate change in America, I decided I could no longer be part of a country that I had given up on when it came to social justice. The people were too complacent and too brainwashed to do anything about an unjust system, and as long as religion and corporations were in control, nothing would ever change, regardless of what political party was in power.

It was then that I decided to leave the USA, and become a citizen of a more just society. I had several countries in mind, but with my Canadian son's encouragement, my wife and I finally decided on Canada.

Canadians are intrinsically happier than Americans, because they know that they live a country that cares; although, there is still room for improvement. Of course, I still look with trepidation whenever I see signs of the Americanization of Canada, especially when U.S. religious groups try to interfere with things like gay marriage, abortion and the separation of church and state. Their attempts to influence Canadian politics is especially appalling to people like me, who came here to escape their stranglehold on the American government. The world has enough influence from a country that preaches love but practices hate.

CHAPTER 12
THE WINDS OF OPPRESSION

The history books of America are filled with tales of exaltation and praise for war-mongering politicians, business tycoons, soldiers, sports icons and others whose accomplishments are vastly overshadowed by those who toil in anonymity to bring a modicum of justice where there is none.

The teachers who struggle to educate children in the ghettos of despair are vanguards in the battle against the worst disease to afflict mankind, poverty. In a society that has no trouble finding money for bombs and bullets, corporate welfare or tax breaks for the wealthy but willingly ignores the plight of the poor, these mighty warriors in the fight against ignorance valiantly stand-up for those forgotten by the politicians who have no compassion. Despite a lack of resources, these gallant centurions attempt, though education, to give the forgotten ones the key to the door that opens into a world of possibilities. Although not a child of the ghetto, I am writing this book today as a result of an inspiring teacher who showed me the beauty of words. The dedication page of this book is not an after-thought, it is a heart-felt appreciative homage to my 12th grade English teacher, Ms. Powell, who helped an adolescent realize his potential. Where would so many of us be today without the teachers who lit that spark of inquiry that led us down the primrose path to a future of innate possibilities, rather than the dark corridors of despair. I have not seen her in nearly 50 years, and I have valiantly tried to located her, just to say thanks for caring and encouraging me to succeed.

FIGHTING FOR JUSTICE

The social workers who fight for the respect and dignity to which all human beings are entitled receive little in compensation and even less in recognition for the job they do. In America, those who strive to lift up humanity are just an after-thought. Their work is not vital in a nation that worships at the altar of greed. When running for President, Mitt Romney even attacked Barrack Obama for being a community organizer, rather than a businessman. Eschewing the financial rewards he would have received from a law firm, defending corporations, to serve the needs of the poor in Chicago somehow makes Obama less American than a tycoon of vulture capitalism. In other words, America does not need a President who cares about people. It needs a President who cares about corporations. After all, according to Romney's famous statement, "corporations are people, too, my friend."

A nurse in the USA is just another corporate slave to the bottom line, as, unlike most other countries, the USA thinks the "private sector" can be more efficient in the delivery of health care. Therefore, the hospitals of America are just another engine of capitalism. The fact that the USA spends twice as much per person as the countries that have socialized medicine and ranks near the bottom in outcomes, does not keep the Republicans from spreading the lies about America being number one in health care. Well, yes it is – if you are rich. Ask the poor how they are treated by a health care system based on the profit motive.

How many nurses work gallantly without fanfare or praise to serve the poor of America who desperately need someone to care about their welfare. Nurses are well aware that the biggest contributor to poor health is not just a physical disease, but a disease that should not be tolerated in a country as rich as the USA – poverty. Poverty is a breeding ground for diseases of the body, mind and spirit

Although, in my opinion, most doctors are grossly over-compensated, there are some doctors who sacrifice financial rewards to serve the needs of the poor. As a young man, I was president of a university in New Orleans. While there, I had the privilege of being associated with a beautiful (both on the outside and the inside) female doctor who was called the "Bourbon Street Angel," because she devoted herself to serving the poor of the area who toiled for miniscule wages in the up-scale restaurants and hotels where the rich dined and stayed and were expected to be served by those who could work in the establishments but could never dream of eating in one or spending the night in one. Some of the hotels and restaurants allowed her to come in certain days of the week and examine their workers in a room set aside just for her. They were too financially mercenary to provide their employees with health insurance, but, for a doctor willing to treat them for free, they could always find an unused storeroom. This woman was 33 at the time, and came from a wealthy family that could not understand why she was not back in New York City, working as a Park Avenue doctor to the rich and famous. However, I understood that she was an unsung hero who saw life as more than the accumulation of wealth and accolades for accomplishments. This was a woman who realized that the rewards of being a doctor could go far beyond mere dollars and cents.

FIGHTING FOR JUSTICE

I must admit that I am somewhat biased against ministers, since I see religion in the USA as a great handicap that locks far too many Americans in the darkness of judgmental arrogance. As one who firmly believes in freedom of religion, as long as that freedom also includes freedom from religion, I have no problem with people worshipping any God they want. I would defend a person's right to worship a head of cabbage if that was what they desired. However, when you force me to worship a head of cabbage, or have the audacity to stand in public and pray to it and expect me to accept it without discontent, you are asking too much. The same thing applies to people who want to invoke the name of Jesus, Mohammad, Buddha, Lord Krishna or any other supposed deity in public. Freedom of religion is just that – freedom to be religious or freedom not to be religious.

Yet, there are some ministers who are genuinely servants of the people, more than they are servants of God. They see their role as lifting up those who are burdened, and do not point the finger of condemnation. Those who minister to the sick, poor, disenfranchised and forgotten of America are genuinely servants of mankind. They see a person's religion as a personal journey, not as a chance to brainwash someone into the strict adherence to a Black Book that seems to lead more people from "the light" than to it.

Americans love to quote its founders and invoke the Constitution. I wonder how many of them have ever even read the Constitution or the Bill of Rights. Most Americans have no idea what the founders, and so-called great leaders, genuinely felt about religion. Most of the founders were Deists and Unitarians who rejected doctrines like the Incarnation. Thomas Jefferson dismissed the Trinity as "incomprehensible jargon." He and other founders made no mention of God in the Constitution, and took pains not to establish an official church on US soil. For the edification of my readers I will share a few comments from people most Americans have great reverence for, and even believe deeply that these men were Christians. The right wing of America is feeding the population gigantic lies about the founders of America, and the populace is simply too lazy to search out the truth.

Benjamin Franklin:

"I have found Christian dogma unintelligible."

James Madison:

"What influence in fact have Christian ecclesiastical establishments had on civil society? In many instances they have been upholding the thrones of political tyranny. In no instance have they been seen as the guardians of the liberties of the people. Rulers who wished to subvert the public liberty have found in the clergy convenient auxiliaries. A just government, instituted to secure and perpetuate liberty, does not need the clergy."

"What influence, in fact, have ecclesiastical establishments had on society? In some instances they have been seen to erect a spiritual tyranny on the ruins of the civil authority; on many instances they have been seen upholding the thrones of political tyranny;

in no instance have they been the guardians of the liberties of the people. Rulers who wish to subvert the public liberty may have found an established clergy convenient auxiliaries. A just government, instituted to secure and perpetuate it, needs them not."

Madison objected to state-supported chaplains in Congress and to the exemption of churches from taxation. He wrote: *"Religion and government will both exist in greater purity, the less they are mixed together."*

"In no instance have the churches been guardians of the liberties of the people. Religious bondage shackles and debilitates the mind and unfits it for every noble enterprise."

George Washington:

"Religious controversies are always productive of more acrimony and irreconcilable hatreds than those which spring from any other cause."

Thomas Jefferson:

Of all the founding fathers, Jefferson was probably the most outspoken when it came to religion. He was particularly disdainful of what he saw as an impediment to liberty. Can you image Americans ever electing him today with views like those below?

"My word for the Bible – dunghill." (A heap of animal dung or refuse. In modern terminology – bullshit.)

FIGHTING FOR JUSTICE

"Christianity is akin to chicanery."

"I have examined all the known superstitions of the Word, and I do not find in our particular superstition of Christianity one redeeming feature. They are all alike, founded on fables and mythology. Millions of innocent men, women and children, since the introduction of Christianity, have been burnt, tortured, fined and imprisoned. What has been the effect of this coercion? To make one half the world fools and the other half hypocrites; to support roguery and error all over the world."

"The clergy converted the simple teachings of Jesus into an engine for enslaving mankind, to filch wealth and power to themselves. They, in fact, constitute the real Anti-Christ."

"The Christian god can easily be pictured as virtually the same god as the many ancient gods of past civilizations. The Christian god is a three headed monster; cruel, vengeful and capricious. If one wishes to know more of this raging, three headed beast-like god, one only needs to look at the calibre of people who say they serve him. They are always of two classes; fools and hypocrites. To compel a man to furnish contributions of money for the propagation of opinions which he disbelieves and abhors, is sinful and tyrannical."

"It does me no injury to say there are twenty gods, or no god."

"Question with boldness the existence of God."

FIGHTING FOR JUSTICE

Thomas Paine:

"Whenever we read the obscene stories, the voluptuous debaucheries, the cruel and torturous executions, the unrelenting vindictiveness, with which more than half the Bible is filled, it would be more consistent that we called it the word of a demon than the Word of God. What poppycock. It is a history of wickedness that has served to corrupt and brutalize mankind."

"Accustom a people to believe that priests and clergy can forgive sins and you will have sins in abundance. I would not dare to dishonour my Creator's name by [attaching] it to this filthy book [the Bible]."

"I do not believe in the creed professed by the Jewish Church, by the Roman Church, by the Greek Church, by the Turkish Church, by the Protestant Church, nor by any church that I know of. My own mind is my own church."

"My country is the world, and my religion is to do good."

John Adams:

"Where do we find a precept in the Bible for Creeds, Confessions, Doctrines and Oaths, and whole carloads of other trumpery that we find religion encumbered with in these days?"

"The doctrine of the divinity of Jesus is made a convenient cover for absurdity."

FIGHTING FOR JUSTICE

"The Government of the United States is not in any sense founded on the Christian religion."

Could you image the below Republicans even being allowed to speak before a party that is supposed to be the one that loves Jesus the most?

Abraham Lincoln:

"The Bible is not my book nor Christianity my profession."

William Howard Taft:

"I do not believe in the divinity of Christ and there are many other of the postulates of the orthodox creed to which I cannot subscribe."

In a nation where people see an image of Jesus on a grilled cheese sandwich, a burrito, an apple and various other objects from a woman's butt (that is one I want to see) to a beer bottle, one has to have serious doubts about the direction the country is headed. As Sigmund Freud said, "religion is comparable to childhood neurosis."

According to Nietzsche, faith means not wanting to know what is true. This book is about people who stood up for truth and justice against often insurmountable odds, and as long as religion is allowed a public forum in the USA, everyone's liberty is at stake, because those who question the status-quo, which includes religion, run the danger of a backlash from those who oppose free-thought.

FIGHTING FOR JUSTICE

It would be very nice if there were a God who created the world and was a benevolent providence, and if there were a moral order in the universe and an after-life, but as Nietzsche also said, "it is a very striking fact that all this is exactly as we are bound to wish it to be. In the long run, nothing can withstand reason and experience, and the contradiction religion offers to both is palpable."

So, I do not want to argue about the existence of God, that is a subject for another book, However, I think that it is imperative for liberty that church and state must always be held separate. Your right to worship your God should never impose on my right to worship mine, or to not worship at all. Liberty means respecting the rights of all, but in the USA, those who do not worship what Americans think is the right God, or who do not worship at all, are constantly having their rights abridged. That is not democracy. That is totalitarianism.

In the USA, anyone who stands against the norm is suspect. I have discussed many people who have stood up to authority and paid a heavy price for it. As a youth, I always tried to be compliant, because I knew that was what adults expected. Just go along and you can get along was my philosophy. However, I was somewhat of a class clown, so I did get in trouble on occasion, but I rarely ever made an overt challenge to authority. Yet, my 12th grade English teacher, Ms. Powell, instilled in me the idea of challenging the norm and not accepting that which might be unjust. To her, those who did not question, did not care about finding the truth.

FIGHTING FOR JUSTICE

A propitious event occurred my senior year that might seem silly to young people of today who are, especially in Canada, much freer that I was as a youth. In the USA, even today, all school children from kindergarten to the 12th grade are expected to stand and dutifully recite the inane Pledge of Allegiance that is used to brainwash the youth into believing in the infallibility of America. Although illegal to force a child to say it, all do for fear of being ostracized or branded a trouble-maker. Just as the Germans went along with rounding up the Jews, because they feared being ostracized, Americans refuse to stand up to the tyranny they can't even see, because they are blinded by enforced patriotism. Teach a child to believe in the infallibility of America, and when they are older, they will line up to be handed a weapon to defend the indefensible ideals of a lie.

A defining moment in my youth was an event that occurred at my high school in North Carolina. At the age of 17, I was exposed to my first real demonstration against those in authority who demand conformity from the populace. Awhile ago, a high school classmate of mine from those days, who was instrumental in teaching me how important it is to stand up for your rights, died, and I wrote a newspaper editorial about his influence on me during this event, and how it helped to solidify a dedication to never bend before the winds of tyranny promulgated by those who keep us in invisible chains. I shall not use his real name, because it might offend some of his family members who, being from the south, might find the political philosophy I am espousing in this book abhorrent.

FIGHTING FOR JUSTICE

As one gets older, reflection on the past becomes an almost daily ritual. Having left my hometown at the age of 17, I thought I had put that part of my life far behind me, but modern communications is like a magnet that pulls the past back, as old childhood chums, university classmates, friends and former colleagues utilize the marvels of the computer age for reconnection to those with whom they shared the joys of youth.

Reaching an age when news of the illnesses and the deaths of childhood friends and acquaintances makes one realize the transitory nature of human existence, a reflection on the past leads to an examination of life as a prosaic of unfinished dreams. We all fear that we have fulfilled the prophecy of Henry David Thoreau that most men lead lives of quiet desperation.

The death of this childhood friend made me serendipitously reflect on my Asheboro, North Carolina High School graduating class, and all the fun I shared with them in my adolescence. When I received an e-mail about the death of my classmate, Billy, I realized that he was one of over a dozen of my 120 classmates who were now gone. Even though I am supposedly retired, as usual, I was busy planning my next book and preparing to coach a hockey game in pursuit of that ever elusive championship. So, I gave little thought to his death at first, just shrugging it off as another in the string of deaths I have gotten used to as I age.

However, as days passed, I began to realize the significance of his death. What follows may lead my readers to initially ask, "what does that have to do with Billy's death" but be patient and I believe you will see the connection I am attempting to make, although I might take circuitous route to make it.

In 2000, when George Bush lost the U.S. Presidential election by over 500,000 votes, but was still appointed President by the United States Supreme Court, due to an antiquated and grossly undemocratic system of electing a leader that would be exceedingly difficult for Canadians to understand, I made a momentous decision. I felt there was no longer any hope for a country that talked about democracy, but had no idea what it really was. I could no longer countenance being a citizen of a nation where healthcare was a privilege rather than a right, where the right of pre-emptive strikes made a mockery of the civilized norms of the way nations are supposed to conduct themselves, and finally, the idea that citizens could sit idly by and enthusiastically support a government that blatantly tortured people was simply against all that I hold dear as a member of the human race.

Seeing my fellow citizens starving on the streets, while George Bush rewarded the rich with unfair tax breaks that were bankrupting the nation, and watching the government squander money on bombs and bullets to make other nations submit to its will, my disillusionment with a country I had served in the Vietnam War made me finally decide to give-up hope for a more just society.

I elected to vote with my feet. Thanks to a son, who is a Canadian citizen, I was able to cross the

FIGHTING FOR JUSTICE

Canadian border and never look back. Today, I am a proud citizen of a country that avoids war at almost all costs, provides all its citizens free healthcare as a human right, offers social amenities that Americans can only dream about and practices a democratic form of government that serves the people rather monolithic corporations.

I did not know it at the time, but today I realize that Billy may well have been a motivating factor in my momentous decision to seek a more just, caring, democratic and compassionate society. He was one of many people in my youth who sowed the furtive seeds of rebellion against a society that demands conformity. Ironically, he did not realize it, nor did I. It took reflection on my high school years and one single event started by Billy that made me realize how important he and the rest of my classmates were in shaping the way I think today. I only regret that the majority of Americans are not willing to stand against the tyranny of repression that they must face every day in a land that had great promise, but sacrificed it all at the altar of conformity.

Billy and I were not real close friends, but in a class of 120, one does know and interact with almost everyone. We had an economics class together, taught by a very large man named Mr. Felton. We took particular delight in causing trouble in his class, not because we disrespected him, but because he was a lively, gregarious man who was even-tempered and enjoyed cutting-up almost as much as his students did. A fun-loving Billy, along with myself and Charles, an impressionable younger student whom we could manipulate, would often conduct clandestine tricks on Mr. Felton. When we would go too far, his verbal admonishments would include the curt "and you boys may provide me with the pleasure of your company after school today."

Ironically, we actually enjoyed staying after-school, as it afforded us an opportunity to socialize awhile longer. One of those after-school days, Mr. Felton left us alone while he went to see Mr. Phoenix, the principal, whom we irreverently referred to as "Turkey." While he was away, the very cute, young English teacher, Miss Powell, whom we all revered, not just because of her good looks, but because of her devotion to her students, came in and asked for Mr. Felton. Telling her he would be right back, we were delighted to see her take a seat by his desk. I had long ago perfected the art of dropping my pencil, so I could bend over and as I picked it up, sneak a quick look at her shapely legs. Just as I was doing it for probably the thousandth time, in walked another English teacher, Mr. Jarrett, whom we had often tried to fix up with Miss Powell. He knowingly gave me a dirty look, as he knew what I was up to. He and Miss Powell conversed. She got up and left with him. As he went out the door, Billy turned to me and said, "look at Mr. Jarrett's shirt."

Mr. Jarrett's shirttail was hanging out over his pants for some unknown reason. Billy jumped to his feet, pulled out his shirttail and said, "hey, maybe girls like guys with their shirttails out." Suddenly, Charles and I pulled out our shirttails and said, "yeah, from now on we wear our shirttails out."

FIGHTING FOR JUSTICE

Today, shirttails dangling about, wildly coloured hair, baggy pants, plunging necklines and bared midriffs are the norm, so it is difficult for my younger readers to imagine a time when things like that would have been considered a sign of rebellion. Yet, at this time, the simple act of pulling your shirttail out was nothing less than subversion. In a regimented society that makes its youth stand and blindly recite the pledge of allegiance with hand over heart every day, this act of rebellion could not be tolerated.

For over a week, our school was in absolute rebellion, as boys and girls walked around with their shirttails out. Finally, "Turkey" called an assembly of the entire school and let us know in blunt, direct language that those who defied the edict to tuck shirttails in would be expelled and maybe even denied the right to graduate. The rebellion was over, but as we filed out of the assembly, Billy turned to me and said, "Wayne, I will put my shirttail in, but this just isn't right."

That event recessed into the darkness of a mind that often works grudgingly these days, but Billy's death reminded me of how important seemingly innocuous incidents in our lives are. My life, for the most part, has been devoid of contact with those whom I shared my adolescence. However, dear Billy, and his fellow defiant revolutionaries in my graduating class, who defied authority by pulling out their shirttails, had a profound influence on my life, without me realizing it until learning of his death. Billy's death led to a crystallization in my mind of just how important he and my fellow adolescent sojourners in that class were to my commitment to always question authority rather than to obsequiously acquiesce to those who expect blind obedience. Just think of how much better off the USA would be today if its citizens had questioned the authority of the Bush Administration that lied it into two un-winnable wars and created an economic tsunami that has nearly obliterated the middle class.

My life has been a kaleidoscope of transformational incidents that solidified my commitment to battle against the forces of oppression and conformity that try to make us all slaves to corporate puppet masters who manipulate and control the governments of the world. Working as a Military Intelligence Analyst in the Pentagon while in the U.S. Army, being a college professor at 24, coaching university hockey teams, and being a university president at 32, I always tried to maintain a balance between the job I was hired to do, and the needs of the workers I was entrusted to supervise.

An inherent love of writing and the occasional publication of a book kept that dream of "going to Hollywood" a distinct possibility in the back of a mind that was still stuck in adolescence. In the 1980's, I finally made it to California, although I was 30 minutes from Hollywood, in the suburbs of Los Angeles, and although I have done some work in the entertainment industry, I never made it big. Maybe it is because I lack talent, but, based upon the junk I see that passes as entertainment today, I prefer to think it is because I do not have the right "connections" that gets one through the doors of those who control the entertainment conglomerates. Again, even Hollywood is an excellent example of how those born to the "right parents" have the doors of opportunity swung open for them while the rest of us wind up getting those doors slammed in our faces. However, my commitment to questioning authority has never wavered in all these years. I did not know it at the time, but Billy and the my classmates planted the seeds of rebellion deep within my psyche.

In all likelihood, I shall never return to Asheboro, North Carolina. However, as I continue in my commitment to fight for justice and fairness in a world where the entitled corporate class rules with the iron fist of repression, I now realize the debt I owe to those rebels from days long past. They did not know it at the time, nor did I, but their simple act of minor rebellion sowed a seed in my mind that grew into a strong tree that stands tall against the winds of oppression.

FIGHTING FOR JUSTICE

EPILOGUE
THE THUNDER ROAD TALE
AND A CRY FOR JUSTICE

I have had a friend since my university days whom I have admired for a variety of reasons. One of those being the fact that he figured out how to be an entrepreneur and survive without being a wage slave. Although I have been an entrepreneur too, I have always made it a point to have an ancillary job here and there in order to assure that I was accumulating retirement benefits and guaranteeing that I could put food on the table for my wife and children. Like so many other people in America, I was always afraid that I would be on the streets with no money and no hope. America is a country filled with people who are only one pay check away from the streets, and unlike other civilized societies, there is no real safety net for these people. I did not get an education for altruistic reasons, I got an education as insurance against a system that was extremely harsh to those who did not have the benefit of a university degree.

I am going to share an interesting story that will be seen by some as an exercise in self-aggrandizement, but I am telling it, because it illustrates an important point that I am about to make. It revolves around the aforementioned friend of mine, who over the course of our university years spent a great deal of time with me.

First, for my younger readers, who may not be familiar with the old days before cable and satellite television, there was a time when most cities only received two or three television signals, and the reception was often very poor. We used to refer to the poor quality of the picture as being snowy. The aforementioned friend of mine was, like me at the time, prone to be politically conservative. For that reason, we got along real well. We were also television addicts, who always scheduled our classes around *The Andy Griffith Show* and *The Beverly Hillbillies* reruns, which came on every day at 11:00 AM. In fact, he loved television so much that one Saturday on a double date, he was in the front seat making-out with a girl, while I was in the back seat, doing something even more exciting with my date. All of a sudden, he shouts, "hey, it is almost 10:00 o'clock, Wayne and I have to get back to the dorm to watch *Gunsmoke*." Now that is true devotion to television.

Since we were in Terre Haute, Indiana at a time when there were only two television stations there, he longed to get access to some of the TV stations in the largest city in Indiana, Indianapolis. We had a large television in the lounge area for everyone to use, but it also only got the two local stations. My friend had a 5 inch Sony television that we used for our personal viewing. In fact, he would often sleep with it at night, cuddled up under his blanket, watching it as I studied or slept.

For many years I had told him about the movie staring Robert Mitchum that had become a southern classic as it had been shot in North Carolina and Tennessee. I would venture to say that even today, there are very few people under the age of 40 in North or South Carolina who have not seen the 1957 film about a Carolina mountain boy who transported illegal alcohol. Before the invention of the VCR or DVD, his only hope to see it was if it ever came on television. To see it almost became an obsession with him; consequently, one day while reading the *Indianapolis Star* newspaper, I happened to look at the television section, and noticed that an Indianapolis television station was showing *Thunder Road* at 5:00 PM. The only problem was that we could not get a strong enough signal to pick up Indianapolis television stations.

When I informed him that *Thunder Road* was on, he was frantic to see it. This led to a frenzy of ideas about how we could watch this movie. At 4:00 o'clock, he even called up two nearby motels to ask of they got Indianapolis television stations, but one was full, and the other only had a room available without television. He determined that he did not have time to drive to Indianapolis, and as I watched him sit in front of the television set, frantically adjusting the rabbit ears (again, for my younger readers, that was an antenna that came out of the top of the TV set) I felt an obligation to make sure he saw something that I had built up as a seminal event in motion pictures over the years we had known one another. It was then that I made a decision that has led to raucous laughter when the tale has been related to countless numbers of people over the years. I told him to sit tight, and not worry. I was going to make sure he saw *Thunder Road*. It was 4:15.

I made a visit to a nearby hardware store and picked up 200 feet of television antenna wire. Taking the elevator back up to the room, two friends who shared the elevator with me asked what I was up to? I replied with cold determination, "I am on a mission from God." It was 4:30.

My heart raced and my face became flush as I looked at my watch and realized I only had 30 minutes until *Thunder Road* time. We were on the 7th floor (Room 727) of a u-shaped 12 story building as indicated below:

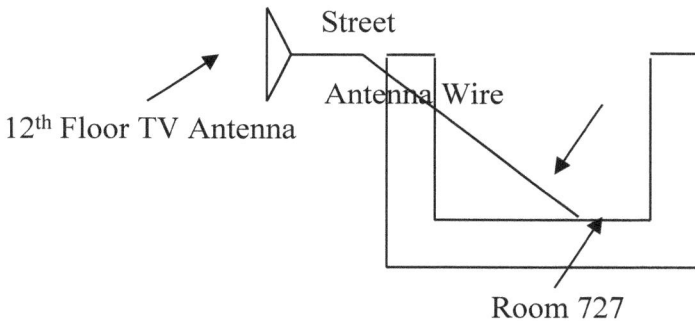

I walked into the room, told my friend to relax as I was about to perform the greatest miracle since Jesus rose from the dead. I informed him I was going onto the roof, and it was his job to toss the antenna wire up to the eight floor, then I would have someone above us pass it up to the ninth and so on, until they got it to me on the roof, where I would simply walk across to the television antenna, hook it up and he could finally see *Thunder Road*.

I had all the people in the rooms above us lined up and ready to execute with delicate precision this feat of daring-do that would make this a day my friend would remember for all time. On the 12th floor, I pried the trap door to the roof open by unscrewing the latch that held the Yale lock. It was a piece of cake. I leaned over and called down to room 1227 and with uncanny athletic finesse I caught the antenna wire on the first try, put it by my hip and proceeded across the rooftop unfurling the wire until I had it hooked onto the antenna. Now, I was ready to hook it onto the 5 inch Sony television, and make my friend the happiest man in Indiana. It was 4:50 PM and things seemed to be running smoothly. Then, upon plugging in the antenna wire, the picture was barely visible but the sound was coming in fine. I told him to extend the rabbit ears, and maybe the combination of antennas would make the picture clearer. It did not work. 4:55 PM and my friend was becoming frantic.

I looked out the open window and remembered something my father had told me as a young child. When the television signal is not clear, move the set closer to a window and the signal should improve. Relying on my father's wisdom, I instructed my friend to carry the TV set near the window. As he did, he looked over his shoulder at me and shouted, "it is coming in better. Oh, yeah, it is definitely coming in much better."

He moved to the window, leaned out of it, extended his hands as far as he could and turned toward me with a slight smile slowly creasing across his lips. "Wayne, grab my legs, I think we have it."

I walked over to him, grabbed his two legs and he crawled on the window sill and hung out on the side of the building clutching the TV. As I leaned my head out holding his legs near his ankles, he said, "lower, Wayne, lower, it is coming in."

Finally, as I stretched out as far as I could, he gleefully proclaimed, "coming in fine, coming in fine. I am watching *Thunder Road*. I am watching *Thunder Road*."

I can only image what people cruising by on the busy street below must have thought when they saw a person hanging out a window with a TV in his hands. At each commercial, I pulled him inside, and he excitingly told me how wonderful I was to make it possible for him to see *Thunder Road*.

After the movie ended, I told him what he had done was foolish, trusting me to hold onto him. He looked me right in the eyes and said, "Wayne, you are one person who has never let me down. I would trust you with my life anytime, anywhere."

I never tire of telling this tale about my friend, because it illustrates how important trust is in a world where trust is constantly abused by those we place in positions of power. How wonderful it would be if we could place our trust in government the way this individual placed trust in me. To this day, it makes me proud to know that someone actually trusted me that much. Are there any politicians in any country that we could put that much trust in today?

That is where Canadians and Americans differ dramatically. In Canada, citizens are not brainwashed into trusting their government to do the right thing. In fact, it is just the opposite. Canadians are taught to mistrust their government and to never take things at face value. Asking questions of your government is a duty of each citizen in Canada. Patriotism is not used by the Canadian government as a means to manipulate and control the population.

Canada had the good sense to stay out of Iraq, because its citizens were too smart to fall for the lies, manipulation and flag-waving patriotic gibberish that made dopes out of the American people.

That is not to say Canada is a perfect country, but Canadians are happier and less stressed than Americans, because they know that they have a government that cares, because the citizens demand it. I can remember being out of work one time in my life, and not having the money to afford health insurance for my wife and the one child that I had then. At that time, I asked myself why I had enlisted in the U.S. Army to serve a country that was not interested in serving me. In Canada, I would not have had to ask myself that question, because my family would have been guaranteed healthcare as a basic right to which all citizens are entitled.

Canada is a country that genuinely insures all its citizens are afforded equal rights. It is a privilege to live in a country where two people of the same sex have the right to marry, regardless of what some pontificating, self-righteous interpreter of God's word might say. How wonderful it is to see people of the same sex being able to show affection for one another in public, rather than having to hide their sexual orientation, because they live in a country controlled by religious bigots who speak of love but do not practice what they preach..

There is only one thing I am sicker of hearing than the endless references to 9/11 in America. That is the phrase, "*family values.*" This is a term that has been part of the Republican mantra for over 30 years now. These people talk constantly about family values, but they never do anything that illustrates a commitment to family values. Isn't guaranteeing health care for every member of a family the apex of family values. Isn't assuring every citizen a living wage an example of family values? Isn't making certain that the rich pay a fair share in taxes family values? Isn't spending more money on education and social amenities than on bombs and bullets an example of family values? Where would these family values preaching morons think their beloved Jesus would stand on issues like these?

Each day, from my mountaintop island hideaway, I look out my office window to gaze over the clear blue bay at the magnificent snow-capped Canadian Rockies that tower over Vancouver 40 kilometres in the distance, and I let out a sigh of relief, knowing that I am finally free of America. Yet, even here, I fear the tyranny promulgated on the world by this bastion of self-righteousness that wants to impose its warped sense of morality and justice on the entire planet, so that its corporate and religious anti-bodies can infect all of humanity with its creed of exploitive, capitalistic, monotheistic dogma that will enslave us all to the evil of greed and theological autocracy.

FIGHTING FOR JUSTICE

I left America, because I got old, tired, discouraged and depressed after years of struggling and hoping for change from a society that looks on change as tyranny. America has been an authoritarian society from its very inception, when it made slavery an integral part of its Constitution while declaring in the same document that "all men are created equal." This hypocrisy is at the very root of all that America stands for in a world that is rapidly seeing it as a country determined to enslave all of humanity to the tyranny of corporate control.

Most Americans would not know what justice was if it bit them on the ass. They are so easily manipulated by the ministers of mayhem who stand in the church pulpits on Sundays that they genuinely believe God is always on America's side. Tell the mindless sheep who are unable to think for themselves that Jesus says red is white and white is red, and Americans shout, "Hallelujah." Then, they fall in line and support a government that maims, kills and destroys so its corporate entities can reap profits while the poor die on the battlefields defending a country that sees them as nothing but cannon fodder.

Americans continue to fall prey to the last refuge of scoundrels – patriotism. Their politicians are not statesmen, they are simply scoundrels marketed like any other product in a capitalistic society. Each campaign hires marketing experts to fool the American people into voting for a candidate based upon the mundane rather than the substantive. Even debates are clouded by pat phrases and guarded responses. The corporate run media never offers any intelligent moderators who are willing to challenge the candidates with tough, probing questions, either because today's broadcast journalists are too poorly trained by their corporate benefactors or are fearful of offending a candidate whom they might want to appear on their shows in the future. Where are today's Walter Cronkites and Dan Rathers, who were true journalists unafraid to challenge politicians no matter what the reaction might be? Cronkite said before he died that he was appalled at he state of broadcast journalism, and Dan Rather was hounded out of his job at a network that was fearful of offending the Bush Administration.

According to the media, and U.S. political leaders, America is a nation of heroes. The firemen and the policemen who died in the World Trade Center were proclaimed heroes. But why is a person who does his or her job a hero? Were they not paid to rescue people in distress? Is that not the very definition of their job? If one followed that line of thought, every man and woman who gets up and goes to work each day is also a hero. What happened to the praise for the gardeners, the assembly line workers, the janitors, the department store clerks and the construction workers? No newsperson dared explore this paradox.

I think one of the best examples of how America makes unlikely heroes out of people is John McCain. Here is a man who was a prisoner of war for 5 ½ years, and there is no doubt that he suffered at the hands of his captors. Of course, his captors were well aware of the fact that he was the son and grandson of Admirals. That fact made them offer several times to repatriate him, and to his credit he refused. Yet, due to his family connections, he was offered the opportunity, and I am sure that he was treated better than the other prisoners as a result of his family background. Even the communists were cowered by those from wealth and power.

According to several reliable sources, after McCain's capture he was bayoneted in the foot and his shoulder was smashed with a rifle butt by the North Vietnamese. After being slapped around for three or four days by his captors who wanted military information from him, he realized that he was in critical condition, so he said he would give military information in return for medical care. When I was in the U.S. Army at the same time as McCain was a prisoner, that very statement was a violation of the Military Code of Conduct. You are supposed to only give your name, rank and serial number. He even went so far as to let his captors know that he was the son of Admiral John S. McCain, the soon to be commander of U.S. forces in the Pacific. That too, was a violation of the Military Code of Conduct.

Do not misunderstand me, had I been captured, I would have spilled my guts, because by then I had begun to realize that the Vietnam War, like the wars in Iraq and Afghanistan, was a war of conquest, conducted by a country intent on making the world a corporate run gulag.

Today, McCain is hailed as a great American hero, but no newsperson would dare ask him a question about his 23 bombing missions over North Vietnam or the aforementioned violations of the Code of Military

Conduct. Did he drop bombs on innocent women and children? Did he destroy hospitals and schools? And how heroic is it to take part in an illegal and immoral war of conquest? Yet, there is no newsperson who would dare pose these questions to him? The real heroes were the ones who refused to serve, many of whom escaped to Canada. In fact, I have run into many of these 60's and 70's refugees on my visits to Salt Spring Island, across the bay from my home, which was a haven for draft dodgers and deserters in those days.

The lack of committed and competent news people, along with virulent patriotic jingoism is what led to the debacle in Iraq. The corporate media was a willing participant in the lies that rallied the American people to support tyranny and injustice launched against a nation that posed no credible threat to the USA. As I watch the moronic babble and cutesiness of today's news programs, I look back on the coverage afforded the Vietnam War, and realize that the media was a servant of the people then, as it constantly exposed the folly of an illegal and immoral war of conquest. Of course, they were not part of corporate conglomerates at the time. Today, the media is a cheerleader for whatever misadventures the USA wants to engage in all across a world that fears the country, rather than respects it.

Many men my age, who served in the military during the Vietnam War were traumatized by their experiences in combat. It was not combat that traumatized me. Rather, it was being stationed in the Pentagon, where, with a top secret security clearance, I became privy to the countless acts of terrorism promulgated all across the globe by the USA. Day after day, I reviewed documents that made me realize that I had been brainwashed as a child into believing in the infallibility of America. Unfortunately, most Americans are still falling for the same lies and deceit utilized to con me into volunteering for a war that was a moral abomination.

The real heroes in America are the many people like those mentioned in this book who have made bold stands against the status quo, and fought for genuine freedom in a country that demands conformity and patriotic servitude from citizens too wrapped up in religion and flag-waving to ever question the veracity of their greed-based system of theocratic servitude. They are the unsung and forgotten who have fought a lonely, desperate, perilous battle against a monolith of corporate and religious evil in a system of economic depravity. Unfortunately, there are far too few people today willing to fight for justice in the land of hypocrisy.

ALSO BY J. WAYNE FRYE
AVAILABLE FROM YOUR BOOKSTORE
OR AMAZON.COM

WHEN JESUS
CAME TO JERSEY
AS THE SON
OF THUNDER
AN AARON ADAMS
ADVENTURE

J. WAYNE FRYE

FIGHTING FOR JUSTICE

TRY THESE BOOKS BY J. WAYNE FRYE
AND JASMINE FALLING RAIN FRYE
ABOUT PEOPLE WHO FOUGHT
AGAINST OPPRESSION.
AVAILABLE FROM YOUR BOOKSTORE
OR AMAZON.COM

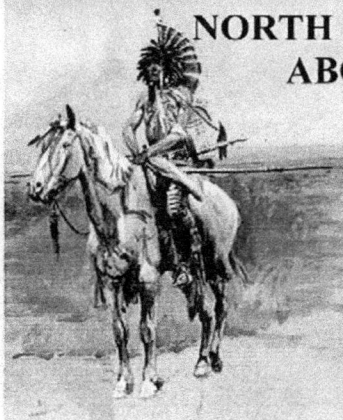

POINTS OF REBELLION

NORTH AMERICAN ABORIGINALS WHO FOUGHT FOR JUSTICE

JASMINE FALLING RAIN FRYE
J. WAYNE FRYE

CANADIAN ANGELS OF MERCY: NURSES IN TIMES OF PERIL 1885-1918

JASMINE FALLING RAIN FRYE
J. WAYNE FRYE

Also Read These Books by J. Wayne Frye

Worth
Fall From Apocalypse
How Hockey Saved A Jew From the Holocaust

FIGHTING FOR JUSTICE

FOR SPORTS LOVERS OF ALL AGES
Available from your local bookstore
or Amazon.com

The *TO KILL A MOCKINGBIRD*
of the 21ˢᵗ Century.

HOCKEY MANIA
AND THE MYSTERY
OF NANCY RUNNING ELK

J. Wayne Frye

With an Introduction
By
Jasmine Falling Rain Frye

The story of an extraordinary hockey team that defied all
the odds one remarkable season, and a player who solved
a murder and helped a beautiful young member of his tribe
find peace in her troubled life.

www.ingramcontent.com/pod-product-compliance
Lightning Source LLC
Chambersburg PA
CBHW050111280326
41933CB00010B/1060

* 9 7 8 0 9 7 3 5 9 7 3 5 6 *